BECOMING A FAMILY

BECOMING A FAMILY

Promoting Healthy Attachments with Your Adopted Child

LARK ESHLEMAN, Ph.D.

TAYLOR TRADE PUBLISHING
Lanham • New York • Oxford

First Taylor Trade Publishing edition 2003

This Taylor Trade Publishing hardcover edition of *Becoming A Family* is an original publication. It is published by arrangement with the author.

Published by Taylor Trade Publishing
An imprint of the Rowman & Littlefield Publishing Group, Inc.
4501 Forbes Boulevard, Suite 200
Lanham, Maryland 20706

Distributed by National Book Network

Library of Congress Cataloging-in-Publication Data

Eshleman, Lark.
    Becoming a family : promoting healthy atttachments wtih your adopted child / Lark Eshleman.
        p. cm.
    Includes index.
    ISBN 0-87833-309-6 (alk. paper)
    1. Adoption. 2. Adoption—Psychological aspects. I. Title. 3. Bonding and Attachment
HV875 .E84 2003
362.73'4—dc21   2003009195

⊗™ The paper used in this publication meets the minimum requirements of American National Standard for Information Sciences—Permanence of Paper for Printed Library Materials, ANSI/NISO Z39.48–1992.
Manufactured in the United States of America.

DEDICATIONS

First, this book is dedicated to my sons, Christopher Ross and Daniel Leigh. Chris is a strong, loving, intelligent, and creative young man who has taught me the *patience and persistence* that healthy attachment love requires. Don't worry, Chris—I know I have more to learn. Danny, who died from this life while I was writing the book, was a young man of nature, music, and beautiful spirit, who taught me unconditional love in its most pure form. My life is as rich and fulfilled as it is because of you, My Loves.

Second, this book is dedicated to the two people who, more than anyone, motivated me to put my learning in the field onto the written page. To Bob Patterson, my friend, colleague, and partner, I give my gratitude and love. To Linda Karasch, my friend, mentor, and inspiration, I offer thanks beyond measure.

Furthermore, this book was written in conjunction with, and aided immeasurably by, Wendy Walker. Wendy, it has been a joy and a pleasure to work and learn with you! She dedicates her fine work in this book to her parents, Jack and Connie Walker.

CONTENTS

Acknowledgments   ix

Preface   xi

PART I: ADOPTION AND ATTACHMENT

1. The Blessings—and Risks—of Adoption   3

2. Professional Evolution of Attachment Theory,   11
   by John A. Biever, M.D.

3. What Does Healthy Attachment Look, Sound,   22
   and Feel Like?

4. Healthy Attachment Interrupted   33

PART II: FOSTERING ATTACHMENT
WHEN YOU WELCOME YOUR NEW CHILD

5. Preparing Your Home   55

6. Bringing Your Baby Home   63

7. Parenting to Enhance Attachment   80

PART III: COPING WTH ATTACHMENT DISORDERS

8. Health Care: Medical Problems from an Attachment Perspective   109

9. School: How to Make It Positive in Your Child's Life   115

10. Therapy: How to Get Professional Help for Children with RAD   134

11. Conclusion   162

Appendix A: Parenting Profile for Developing Attachment   165

Appendix B: Resources   169

Glossary   173

Bibliography   177

Index   181

About the Author   187

ACKNOWLEDGMENTS

There is no way that this book could have been written without the consistent and enthusiastic writing, organization, and emotional support of Wendy Walker. Her writing skills have been key to making the often difficult concepts and complex problems understandable so they can be avoided or solved. Her thirst to understand what healthy attachment and attachment problems are all about has been crucial in my ability to order my own learning, teachings, and thoughts into what I hope is a practical treatise on how to help adoptive families. Wendy, here's to you and all that you have done to enlighten the lives of countless numbers of deserving, appreciative people—me among them!

Bruce Mowday completed the critically important job of finding the "just right" editor and publisher for a book such as this that is written for a particular audience. Thank you, Bruce, for your practical and always calm work in putting me together with Taylor Publishing and introducing me to Wendy.

John Biever, M.D., did what I have trouble doing—writing a concise and accurate history of this field to date. He is a consummate educator, and I am happy he is in the field to help us all learn.

Michael Emmerich, too, my editor at Taylor Publishing, had the grace to tell me when I was "too long" and when I was "too technical" and, of course, when I was "just right." For his family's own journey, and for guiding me on mine, thanks and very best wishes, Mike!

Lynn Weber, my final "light" editor, did so much to organize my sometimes scattered thoughts. Lynn, thank you for knowing how to make more clear what Wendy and I were trying to say.

The children with whom I have worked over the years have guided me in learning to understand and help heal their battered, frightened, yet strong and loving souls and minds. Thank you for trusting me to be close to you as we made our journeys together. I especially thank the wisdom and guidance of Elizabeth Goff, M.D., and the Coleman family. However, each and every family has given me inspiration beyond measure! I thank and applaud you all and hold you close in my heart.

The colleagues with whom I work and from whom I continue to learn are too numerous to cite on this page. I refer to some in the book, specifically to those who add to the development of our synergistic trauma and attachment therapy. I need to note specifically Phyllis Booth, Linda Eisele, John Jarvis, Robin Karr-Morse, Vicky Kelly, Jeff Klunk, Vicky Neely, Susan and Siegried Othmer, Linda Shope, Mary Sourber, John Tardibuono, and Martha Welch. Every aspect of my work is profoundly enriched by my colleagues and staff at the Institute for Children and Families, especially Bob Patterson, Kathy Twardowski McBeth, Kathy Caruso, Liz Maxey, Kate Nolt, Ellen Guinan, Carolyn Schleuter, Leslie Higgins , and Toby Spinelli. The Board of ATTACh, also, has been extraordinarily supportive and helpful.

And, of course, family and close friends are the mainstay and inspiration for all of our best work. I give all credit and gratitude to my family from Upstate New York, the entire Eannace-Phillips-Infusino-Cianciolo "clan," and my friends and family in Lancaster, Pennsylvania, especially John Eshleman, Tony and Elaine Ugolnik, Jil Trainer, Marge Roy, Mary Steffy, Sue Custley, Harold Wenger, and Rob Gillio—and to Bert Patterson for her unwavering, motherly support through my own times of crisis.

PREFACE

This period will be one of the most exhausting, stressful but magical times in your life. Parenting is an art, and we all have to feel our way as we go. . . . A healthy secure attachment between you and your child will be the foundation of your relationship through the years and be of great benefit to your child's future mental health and happiness.

—MOTHER OF TWO GIRLS ADOPTED FROM CHINA

Congratulations! You are among the thousands of Americans and others around the world who are thinking of adopting, perhaps internationally. You may see adoption as an opportunity to make a positive contribution to the world. You may want a child to enter your life so you can love and be loved in this most intimate and giving of ways. You may decide you want to "give birth" in your family without actually conceiving a child. Whatever your reason for exploring this exciting, life-altering possibility, I hope you will find this book informative, supportive, helpful, and a positive addition to your loving adventure.

Throughout this book you will read about the experiences, positive and negative, that families have had with adoption. The book was originally conceived to be specific to issues of international adoption; you will see special attention in places to this international adoption experience.

However, there quickly seemed enough reasons to expand the scope of the book to include issues relating to both domestic and international adoptions.

These families with whom I have been fortunate to work and from whom I learn so much share my belief that it is essential to know *before an adoption* as much as possible about what may happen and to put into place all possible ways of encouraging the healthy attachment and healing that can and should happen. This will give the best chance for you and your young one to quickly develop into a happy, healthy, and loving family.

WHY ADOPTION?

Adoption is a big business and is growing each year. Parents relate to me a multitude of reasons for exploring this option of family planning, among which are the following (in no particular order of importance or frequency):

- Desire to relieve the suffering of a child who may not otherwise have a chance to grow up in a loving, nurturing environment
- Inability to bear children due to fertility or obstetric problems or age
- Spiritual or religious calling to help others in need
- Single parenting
- Same-sex couple
- Desire to raise a child who shares your ancestry
- Wish to expand your family without going through pregnancy and delivery again
- Desire to choose the sex of your child
- Simple desire to have a child to love

I think that the popularity of adoption, and especially international adoption, has at least something to do with our American nature of being big-hearted and generous, loving people—certainly most admirable traits in my view. As long ago as 1837, Alexis de Tocqueville described Americans as the most peculiar people in the world. "You'll not believe it when I tell you how they behave. In a local community in their country a citizen may conceive of some need which is not being met. What does he do? He goes across the street and discusses it with his neighbor. Then what happens? A committee comes into existence and then the committee begins functioning on behalf of that need. And you won't believe this but it is true. All of this is done without reference to any bureaucrat. All of this is done by the private citizens of their own initiative" (quoted in Gannon and associates 1994).

In this case, Americans are seeing the plight of children not their own, perhaps even in other parts of the world, and are responding with their big hearts. Who can forget the pictures of beautiful, big-eyed, dark-haired children in orphanages in Romania several years ago? Programs to help children around the world, by sending aid to them or by bringing them here, have existed in some form or other for centuries in the United States. It seems de Tocqueville was right about our "meeting a need" nature!

WHO I AM

So as you consider adopting a child and read more about the process, or if you are already an adoptive parent and wondering about what is happening (or not happening) in the area of attachment with your own young one, you might ask, "Why should I read *this* person's book? Of all the people out there who write or teach or counsel about adoption, what does *this* person have to share that could be helpful or valuable to me and my family? How do I know to trust her judgment?"

I offer this short section about myself because it is important for you to be able to evaluate my background and credentials when you decide whom to trust and whose advice to follow. I am first and foremost a part of a family. For me, the family is where it all begins and where we all can gain our greatest emotional strength and wisdom. My own children have taught me more about life than anyone. In fact, my son Chris has accused me more than once of going into the field of psychology to "figure him out"—and I have learned and continue to learn from all the children in my family, old and young, immediate and extended.

Professionally I am a child, adolescent, and family psychotherapist, having earned a Ph.D. in clinical psychology in 1998. My expertise is working with children who have experienced early trauma, attachment difficulties, or abuse. I became a certified school psychologist in Pennsylvania in 1994, am board certified in domestic violence by the

American Academy of Experts in Traumatic Stress, and have had exciting, fulfilling careers as an elementary school principal for almost ten years and as a children's librarian.

As I write this book I am the clinical director of the Institute for Children and Families (ICF), an organization I founded in West Chester, Pennsylvania, in 2000. ICF is a leading center for treating children and adolescents who suffer from the lasting effects of early trauma or from serious and destructive breaks in the bonding or attachment process between child and parent. (For information about our ongoing work at the Institute, see our website at www.instituteforchildren.com.)

In my work I have come in personal and therapeutic contact with children from around the world who have suffered the fearful, painful, and neurologically damaging effects of war and other forms of organized violence. I spent almost a year in the Balkans after their 1991–1995 war working with mental health relief organizations and professionals. As part of my doctoral work, I was instrumental in securing over $450,000 in grant money from Rotary International, the Rotary Club of Lancaster (Pa.), and the Holloman-Price Foundation, among other groups, to create and implement services and professional training programs to expand a major children's emotional relief effort for children around the world impacted by war, natural disasters, and other community trauma. The center we began in the Balkans during that time continues to help children and their families in this region.

Among my publications is a community-based response program, *Healing Emotional Trauma: Treating the Wounded Child* (Eshleman 2000), created specifically for children ages three to ten years old who have been affected by war and other community trauma. In spring 1999 I was fortunate enough to be included in a group of professionals from around the country invited by attorney general Janet Reno and Health and Human Services secretary Donna Shalala to be a member of their "Safe from the Start" task force in Washington, D.C. The purpose of our group was to generate strategies to prevent child exposure to violence and promote public awareness of the harm of children being exposed to (not just being the victim of) violence, especially in their families.

I have also been fortunate to have worked with Linda Karasch and her exceptional crew at CVP Communications (West Chester, Pa.) to produce an award-winning video titled *Attachment Disorder: Solving the Puzzle*. This video, produced in 2001, is designed for use by academicians, clinicians, parents, teachers, adoption professionals, and those who work within the judicial system to learn about the highly misunderstood reactive attachment disorder.

While I maintain a busy practice at the Institute, I remain committed to preventing what are often referred to as "adverse childhood experiences" (for information on this topic, see Anda et al. 2001, 2002; Karr-Morse and Wiley 1997). I serve on the board of directors of several nonprofit organizations, including ATTACh (Association for Treatment and Training in the Attachment of Children). I also spend part of my professional time teaching and training others, especially as we gather important new information about how best to help children relax into being healthy, happy, and developmentally all that they can be.

I grew up in Utica, New York, an area in which many members of my large and loving family of origin still live. For the past almost thirty years my family and wonderful friends and colleagues have lived and worked together in southcentral and southeast Pennsylvania.

This book evolved because I have heard over and over from adoptive parents, "Why didn't anyone ever tell us?" or "If we had only known, we could have made it better for our child and for us!" I hope that this book will provide current and prospective parents with the most up-to-date information available about the process of attachment, the possible barriers that can block attachment from happening easily, ways to encourage and enhance the attachment process, and what to do if there is a problem that requires special attention.

WHAT THIS BOOK COVERS

The focus of this book is on supporting attachment with your new child from day one. There are plenty of good books that will supply you with nuts-and-bolts information about how to navigate through the adoption process: selecting an adoption agency, choosing a country, going through home visits from social-service agencies, making arrangements for your child's citizenship, and the like. In this book we touch on those issues, but only in light of how they affect attachment.

Part I is intended to give you an idea of just what attachment is and why it is so important. Chapter 1 focuses on the process of adoption and how critical attachment is to that process. Chapter 2, written by psychiatrist John Biever, describes the theory behind "reactive attachment disorder," the diagnostic name given by the American Psychiatric Association in its *Diagnostic and Statistical Manual* (2000). Chapter 3 discusses the characteristics of normal attachment between a parent and child—what it is and what it should look and feel like. Chapter 4 shows what can happen when the attachment process is seriously interrupted, for any of a number of reasons, and how this can create an actual change in the child's brain. We use case studies and medical research to show how the neurological damage that these children have suffered then affects their behavior.

Part II presents ways in which you, as an adoptive parent, can help your child avoid attachment problems (or at least minimize them). Chapter 5 discusses the psychological and physical preparation that you can do even before your baby arrives. Chapter 6 deals with a very exciting time—the moment you bring your baby home—and how you can create the most supportive environment into which to bring your little one. You'll also learn what *not* to do during these first days and weeks. Chapter 7 discusses parenting methods that you can use to enhance attachment once your child has settled in. Some of my recommendations will not make sense at first, but please read on! There's a solid, scientific reason for them, trust me.

Part III highlights the practical steps you can take to alleviate your child's attachment problems if you discover your child does indeed have them. Chapter 8 deals with medical problems. I do not go into depth about treating medical issues in this chapter, as this is not a medical text. But providing appropriate medical care is a good way of showing your child that you will keep him or her safe. This chapter also discusses the medical and mental health insurance problems that many parents have encountered and some possible ways to advocate for your child to get what she and your family need and deserve. Chapter 9 discusses schooling, how parents can negotiate with school districts to get the help their children need, and the various alternatives, such as home schooling, that may be best for your children at some point in their education. Chapter 10 talks about professional interventions for children with attachment disorders—everything from diagnosis to the broad range of available treatments.

Finally, the conclusion discusses some "posttherapy" issues that can affect the lives of adopted children. It also talks about the future of attachment therapy, which is, after all, still in its infancy.

Throughout this book you will find many first-person accounts written by adoptive parents and children. I have obtained permission from all of these parents and children to reprint their words and am enormously grateful for their generosity. The names that I will use in this book are pseudonyms. I also use "him," "her," "he," and "she" interchangably.

One last item of housekeeping. Throughout the book you will find words or terms that may be new or seem confusing. These may be terms that are only now being defined in the field or ones that would take on a different meaning if used in another context. If you encounter terms you'd like explained further, or any term in italic, check the glossary in the back of the book for a further explanation. I have tried my best to make this book easily understood and free of professional jargon. However, some words and terms are helpful for you to know, so bear with me, check the glossary, and talk with the medical or mental health professional with whom you work if you're still not sure of the meaning.

I

ADOPTION AND ATTACHMENT

1

THE BLESSINGS—AND
RISKS—OF ADOPTION

To all of you who are thinking about adopting a child—domestically or from a foreign country—to all of you who have chosen adoption as a way of adding to your family, and to all of you who are struggling with aspects of being parents in an adoptive family, this is a book about understanding, knowledge, and empowerment. It is a book about knowing how to make your little one's life and your life happier, safer, more loving, and more secure. This is a book to expand your circle of love and the reciprocal nature of attachment. Believe me, there are few things in the world more beautiful and fulfilling than the true joy of loving and being loved by a child.

But adopting a child is not without risks, and this book is about how to deal with one of the most common risks in adoption: the occurrence of symptoms of a disorder called reactive attachment disorder, which can occur with children who have suffered traumatic breaks in bonding or a lack of normal parental attachment in their early lives. As I discuss the causes, behaviors, and problems associated with attachment issues or the full-blown disorder, some of you may hear a negative tone in the book, something that you did not expect to hear. It might make you angry, and you may conclude that I, as the author, am "just a negative person." You may be frightened and begin to think that adoption is more than you bargained for. But please remember this: I work with many children and families who began their journey of love without the information and tools they needed to make their new family as happy as possible. The result was that they faced often *unnecessary* problems and heartache along the way. My hope and prayer is that this book will give you that information and empower you with those tools to support you on your journey and to increase the chances that the easiest, most loving road will be yours.

ADOPTING, DOMESTICALLY OR INTERNATIONALLY, AND THE RISK OF ATTACHMENT DISORDER

I am making an assumption in this book, and I want to state it up front: I am assuming that you and your adopted child will not have a biological bond. I am assuming that you will not be meeting your child from the loving arms of his or her birth mother and that there has been a break in the natural bond between mother and child. Therefore, I am assuming that your adopted child is at risk for problems associated with attachment and emotional trauma.

Not all children who are adopted internationally or domestically, from orphanages or other agencies, have reactive attachment disorder or posttraumatic stress disorder. But does adopting a child who has had a break from his or her birth mother mean your child has a higher-than-average chance of developing problems related to attachment and trauma issues? I believe that it does, and research suggests that I am right. Is that a reason not to adopt, especially internationally? I don't believe so.

But parents need to know that, increasingly, agencies and even countries that cannot care for children given up in their early life, especially children who have experienced early trauma and are further traumatized by poor institutional care, are being put forth as being healthy and "just needing love." You may be one of the loving, unsuspecting, and eager families who may have waited a long time to bring your little one into your family. Or you may have been led to believe that the only thing you have to be concerned about is whether the child waiting for you is medically or physically sound or healthy. (See table 1 for a list of the most common concerns of parents before and after adoption.)

However, the sad stories of far too many families, and new medical information, have shown us that for thousands of families, adequate medical information wasn't available. Or psychological or emotional difficulties were not evident or shared with the family. It could be that a troubled or abusive history was not revealed to new parents, who, had they known, might have decided not to adopt or might well have sought treatment immediately after adoption. Too many families are told, "Just wait. Give it time. It will work out by itself."

Love alone is not enough to heal some of the types of actual neurological or psychological damage suffered in infancy and early childhood. You may need to learn new types of specialized parenting skills, some of which will seem completely counterintuitive. Without this knowledge, parents repeatedly and unnecessarily suffer the heartache of watching their children grow up with neurological and behavioral difficulties.

While writing this book, I worried that some of the parents' experiences would come across as too negative and might scare off some prospective parents. You need to understand that adopted children are only *at risk for* attachment problems. What if your child doesn't turn out to have an attachment problem? Great! Taking the steps I recommend to enhance attachment with your child will certainly not hurt him or her in any case. If an attachment problem does emerge, being knowledgeable about attachment may help the situation, and you'll know that getting help early can prevent the heart-wrenching situations that all too often bring families with already grave problems to my office door.

TABLE 1
PARENTAL CONCERNS ABOUT ADOPTION

Before Adoption	After Adoption
Potential medical problems: 94%	Medical problems: 18%
Developmental delay: 31%	Developmental delay: 10%
Behavioral problems: 18%	Behavioral, emotional, or social issues: 72%

(Adapted from Mainemer 1998)

Remember, too, that it is never too late to enhance a relationship, even if there have been problems for quite some time. While the issue of addressing long-standing damage is not the goal of this book, I can tell you that I have worked with many wonderful people who have been trying to heal their families for many years, often using the ineffective approaches. The right techniques, parenting skills, and therapy *can* help.

WHY I USE "MOM": THE FIRST SOURCE OF ATTACHMENT

For several reasons, I use the word "Mom" throughout this book to refer to the mother, father, or primary caregiver of an adopted child. Partly this is for the sake of convenience: in a book about parenting, it would be cumbersome indeed to write "mother, father, or primary caregiver" every time I refer to the person with whom the child is going to first attach!

There's another reason for the use of "Mom," and that's because biologically the mother is the child's first attachment figure. Beginning at conception and throughout pregnancy, a child's first biological bond is with his or her birth mother. She is the biological "safety net" that the child uses to know where he or she is safe and where to go for nurturance, food, love, and comfort, to learn about the new world, and to provide help in an emergency. We know this through the many experiments that have been done exploring what is normal, healthy behavior on the part of neonates, infants, and children. Babies know their mother's smell even at birth, long before they are motivated to seek out anything else outside the womb.

Babies have to figure out how to survive in the pretty hostile world into which they are thrust, and these survival skills are part of the bonding process that is intrinsic to babies. In fact a baby's health, relative to sucking, grasping, and similar behaviors, is assessed by hospital personnel in the delivery room minutes after birth using the *Apgar Scale*.

Attachment, in other words, is an instinctive drive. But the process itself is not instinctive; it is learned. It is a more advanced part of the developing brain where babies learn if they are safe or unsafe and where and to whom they must go to have their needs met.

What is the connection between bonding and attachment? It's still not completely understood. If a baby's bonding experience is solid, if he or she consistently feels secure, well connected, and cared for as a neonate and infant, a template of safety and security is established in his or her nervous system. The child learns to believe, "The world is a safe place, and I am safe in it. My needs will be met, as my mom is here to take care of me." The stage is set for the child to then share and transfer this trust to other people. The baby's trust in Mom can be expanded beyond those immediate few people who have proven by their actions that they are safe. From the initial and primitive bonding experience, the child transfers his or her ability to trust Mom to trusting others, such as Dad, Grandmother, or Nanny. Eventually, and through literally thousands of repeated postive, affirming experiences, the baby feels that same level of safety with this expanding circle.

Imagine the countless numbers of times a baby's needs are addressed on a regular basis. The baby is hungry, and is fed. He is wet, and is cleaned and dried. She is anxious, and is rocked and soothed. He is cold, and is covered and warmed. She is ill, and is cared for medically. He falls, and is picked up; she bumps herself, and "Mommy will kiss the boo-boo." These interactions make up the daily routine of well cared-for babies around the world and make up the first-year attachment cycle (see figure 1).

FIGURE 1
FIRST-YEAR ATTACHMENT CYCLE

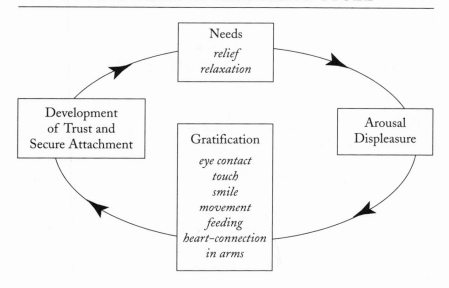

ATTACHMENT DISORDER: A BROKEN BOND

What if that initial bond doesn't form or is broken? What if the child is removed from Mom? When that happens, the infant is at risk for not having the "trust template" fully formed and thus has greater difficulty learning the critical experience of becoming attached.

Imagine having your first, most important relationship with Mom disrupted while you were an infant or toddler—no one, or at least not Mom, to tuck you in at night, to smile at your first steps, or to keep you safe from monsters. Perhaps this most important person, your mom, was emotionally unavailable. Or perhaps, even worse, she was the actual source of neglect or abuse. You start to view yourself as worthless and unlovable, your mom as untrustworthy, and the world as unsafe.

Attachment disorder or difficulties can happen when the vital first relationship between the infant and mother is disrupted for a prolonged period (see table 2). This disruption may be due simply to having multiple caregivers, to illness (either the child's or the parent's), to neglect, abuse, or anxiety, or to addictions or depression of the primary caregiver. Without a strong, healthy first relationship, many other difficulties can occur.

Children with attachment issues may not develop emotionally as we would hope and expect. *Hypervigilance* and control issues replace trust

TABLE 2
COMMON CAUSES OF ATTACHMENT DISORDER

- Physical, sexual, or emotional abuse
- Abandonment by or traumatic separation from primary caregivers
- Separation from mother or primary caregivers, including extreme family stress or mother's postpartum depression
- Neglect, including ineffective and incompetent parenting
- Inconsolable pain, such as recurring ear infections or pain associated with medical interventions
- Frequent changes in homes or caregivers
- Pre- and perinatal insults, such as exposure to drugs and alcohol in utero or birth trauma

(Adapted from Institute for Children and Families, LLC)

in caregivers. Children may become frightened if they sense any danger of losing control of the environment. They become locked in the states of fight, flight, or freeze (Perry 2001, 2002). School issues, poor peer interactions, developmental delays, sensory issues, and certainly self-concept (how you *see* yourself), self-esteem (how you *feel* about yourself), self-pride, and hygiene are potential problems. Parents become stressed from dealing with a child who avoids the warmth of emotional intimacy at all costs. Or they become exhausted with the clinging, fearful state from which this child finds he or she cannot escape.

Preventing or providing interventions for early difficulties with attachment is what this book is all about.

ATTACHMENT TERMINOLOGY

Throughout this book you will meet words that are used in ways that you don't usually see them. If a word seems strange or used in an unusual way, or if you don't understand it from the context, or if the word is in italic, check the glossary of terms in the back of the book.

The terms "attachment disorder," "attachment issues," and "reactive attachment disorder" (RAD) are not interchangeable. However, as a parent you don't need to be overly concerned about the fine distinctions between them, partly because even professionals in the field do not yet agree on their exact definitions. Reactive attachment disorder of infancy or early childhood is the psychiatric diagnostic name; in the American Psychiatric Association's *Diagnostic and Statistical Manual-IV-TR* (2000) it is defined in section 313.89. It is the most narrow term and has the most strict criteria. "Attachment issues" suggests that the child is not totally in sync with the mother; these issues are considered significant if they are severe enough to interfere with the child's or family's life. "Attachment disorder" is not the same as RAD but includes severe and pervasive impairments in attachment, seriously dysregulated state of being, or dangerous behaviors.

Again, it is not terribly important for parents to use the "right" terminology, as even professionals disagree at this point. What is important is to learn from resources that explain things in ways that make sense to you and, if necessary, to find a professional you can trust.

ABOUT ALEXANDRA + KRISTINA

It is hard to believe that our daughter, Alexandra, has only been here for eight years. It seems like we have always known her. Today she is a very different child than the little five-year-old who arrived from Russia scared and hungry. She has grown into a beautiful young girl who is outgoing, has many friends, and is firmly attached to us.

It was not always so. In the beginning she was indiscriminately affectionate and hated to be touched or make eye contact with us. After allowing her to regress, as our home study agency recommended, and letting her reexperience cuddling and nurturing with her new family, she slowly began to bond. Sensory integration therapy helped her to calm down and enjoy being touched and nurtured. The arrival of a younger adopted sibling was the beginning of an even deeper attachment as she observed her little sister begin her own bonding process. Although she still faces challenges in the classroom due to learning disabilities, she loves school and has progressed tremendously. She is a creative girl who is a wonderful artist and an enthusiastic dancer. It is a joy to watch her grow and mature into a successful young woman.

Alexandra's adoptive sister, Kristina, arrived from Russia as a starving three-year-old. She had known the love of a biological grandmother, so her bonding process progressed quickly, especially since we had learned how to rock and cuddle our older daughter to facilitate bonding. Our Russian facilitator had joked that Kristina was a genius. Of course we thought she was exaggerating, but we were soon to find out that Kristina is truly gifted. Soon after her arrival home she began speaking thirteen- and fourteen-word sentences in English, and she hasn't stopped talking or learning since! She has a zest for life and is like a ray of sunshine in all of our lives. Now, four years after her arrival, she has skipped a whole grade in reading and aspires to be a veterinarian. I have no doubt with her determination and love of learning that she will accomplish her goals.

PROFESSIONAL EVOLUTION OF ATTACHMENT THEORY

By JOHN A. BIEVER, M.D.

A basic understanding of attachment theory and its evolution can be helpful for parents of domestic and international adoptees and for their support team of relatives, friends, and professionals. Our theoretical understanding of the nature of healthy and troubled attachments between children and parents is still in a rather early stage of development when compared with what we have learned about child psychological and social development in general. Nevertheless, we already benefit from some key discoveries and principles of great practical applicability. In this chapter, we shall become acquainted with those current fundamentals of attachment theory and then see how they can enlighten our approach to fostering healthy child development. Then we shall home in on the implications of attachment theory for adoption.

FUNDAMENTALS OF ATTACHMENT THEORY

Throughout the history of humankind, students of human nature have endeavored to understand how children develop their individual personalities, including their unique ways of relating to parents, other adults, and peers. Prior to the beginning of the twentieth century, a popular belief held that at birth each infant is a *tabula rasa*, or "blank slate," ready to be molded into just about any personality shape or form deemed desirable by his parents and possible in his environment. Then began the age of modern investigators of the development of the human mind, most notably the Austrian psychiatrist Sigmund Freud. His insights and discoveries led the way toward general acceptance of the following principles of early childhood development:

- From birth the infant is anything but a tabula rasa, but is instead an active and influential participant in the endless series of interactions with her mother and others, which ultimately will form her personality. The infant's style of interaction is shaped by her genetic makeup, a broad array of factors affecting the quality of her experiences in the womb and during birth, and her experiences during the first crucial months of life.
- Nevertheless, parental factors have a great and enduring impact on the psychological and social development of the child, especially during the first years of life.
- Those parental factors include the current emotional stability and resiliency of the parents and, perhaps even more important, their own vast set of memories of *being* children and *having* parents— in other words, the parents' own attachment experiences.
- Later in life, the thoughts, feelings, and behavior of persons are profoundly affected by early life experiences, for better or for worse. However, those formative life experiences that occur prior to about two or three years of age cannot be remembered consciously, as can later experiences. Instead, if the very early experiences were negative, their impact shows up in the form of feelings, mood states, physical symptoms, strange perceptions, or behaviors unsuitable to current circumstances.

The British psychiatrist John Bowlby was trained in the psychoanalytic tradition founded by Freud. In the aftermath of World War II, he was moved by the plight of certain boys in institutions who showed tendencies toward antisocial behavior and uniformly tumultuous relationships with adults. In researching their early life histories, he found that they all had extremely traumatic beginnings, involving loss of parents, abuse, or neglect. This propelled Bowlby into a professional lifetime of research and writing that yielded the foundation of modern attachment theory. Among his seminal contributions are the following principles:

- The infant's drive to attach to mother is *inborn*, and therefore a full set of attachment behaviors is already present in the infant at birth. Theretofore, Freud had suggested that infants attach to their mothers only after discovering that they are desirable and reliable as attachment figures.
- The ability to achieve and maintain satisfactory attachments remains important throughout life, and the adult's attachment style—including that of her attachment to her own children—is largely determined by the nature of her earliest attachments.
- When separated from their mother or mother equivalent under unusual circumstances, such as when hospitalized, older infants and toddlers typically go through a three-part sequence of emotional reactions: *protest, despair,* and *detachment.* If not successfully reunited with the mother or at least united successfully with a surrogate mother figure, the child eventually essentially goes on with life as usual, but almost as though the mother never existed. Typically, if reunited with the mother during the phase of detachment, the child is coldly indifferent to her.

Carrying forth Bowlby's ideas into systematic clinical observations of mothers and their infants, child psychologist Mary Ainsworth identified three attachment styles of older infants and toddlers to their mothers (Ainsworth 1978). Later, child psychologist Mary Main identified a fourth style (Main and Solomon 1986). The four styles are briefly summarized here:

- Secure: When reunited with the mother after a brief separation in a clinical situation, the securely attached toddler will happily go to mother, receive some "emotional refueling," and then go back to play.
- Insecure/avoidant: When reunited with the mother, the insecure/avoidant toddler will ignore the mother's presence and go on playing as though she were not there.
- Insecure/resistant: When reunited with the mother, the insecure/resistant toddler will cling onto her, showing a mixture of anxiety and anger, and refuse to leave her to return to play.
- Disorganized/disoriented: When reunited with the mother, the disorganized/disoriented toddler will show chaotic behavior, such as spinning or wandering around randomly in the room, showing a range of strong negative emotions.

Currently researchers are studying the ways in which these early attachment styles affect the child's overall emotional health later in life and specifically his ability to form healthy relationships. They have already learned that those with the disorganized/disoriented attachment style are especially vulnerable to psychiatric illness later on. Fortunately, infants with an impaired attachment style with the mother or mothering figures are sometimes capable of a healthier style of attachment with other significant caregivers at the same time, thereby forming a potential alternative model for healthier attachments later in life.

Main and her colleagues have also identified what they refer to as "states of mind with regard to attachment" in adults, which resemble the four infant categories of attachment style. The key features of these "states of mind" relevant to parenting and adoption are that they are born out of the adult's memories of significant attachments with caregiving figures during childhood and that they greatly influence the adult's perceptions and feelings about her children and about parenthood. In fact, studies have demonstrated that children strongly tend to have an attachment style corresponding to their parent's attachment style. Thus, children of parents with the *autonomous/secure* attachment style tend to develop secure attachments to those parents. Those with parents possessing the *dismissing* style tend to be insecure/avoidant in attachment style. Those with parents of the *preoccupied* state of mind regarding attachment tend to be insecure/resistant in attachment style. And children of parents with the *unresolved with regard to attachment* state of mind tend toward a disorganized/disoriented attachment style.

As noted, we already know that toddlers with a disorganized/disoriented attachment style are especially vulnerable to significant mental illness later on in life. Research is incomplete regarding vulnerabilities to mental illness of children with the other types of insecure attachments. However, we can say with confidence that their capacity to form fulfilling relationships is at least somewhat adversely affected by their attachment style. Specifically, avoidantly attached children tend, as the word suggests, to remain emotionally distant from others, making it difficult for caregivers to "read" their needs and respond to them—and making it equally difficult for them to read the needs and meanings of others, including parents. Resistantly attached children tend to develop overly clingy relationships with caregivers, with the ironic combination of difficulty with separations and frequent angry demands when together.

Finally, modern scientific inquiry into the development and function of the human brain is helping to explain why serious deprivations or abuses of the infant often have such lasting adverse effects, but also why substantial recovery remains possible. As mentioned earlier, very early traumatic experiences *are* stored in the brain, although later inaccessible to conscious memory, and can so adversely affect one's ability to accurately perceive and relate to others later on. However, the human brain retains a feature called *plasticity* throughout life. Plasticity is what we use whenever we learn and remember something new. Because of brain plasticity, we have the potential not to erase negative, unconscious early memories, but nevertheless to neutralize their damaging effects on our current and future perceptions and feelings about other people. Psychotherapy can help. For example, while Billy can never consciously recall his father's repeated beatings of his mother in his presence during his infancy, he can nevertheless establish in therapy a connection between that experience and his present tendency to become enraged at his adoptive father's minor disagreement with his mother. He can understand the rage as, in part, the evocation in his mind of the helplessness he must have felt as an infant. He can then learn—because of the plasticity of his brain—to see *and feel* his father, himself, and the current situation more realistically and therefore to respond effectively.

IMPLICATIONS FOR HEALTHY CHILD DEVELOPMENT

The story of humankind is a story of endless separations and reattachments. The fantasy of "independence" is well known to anyone who truly becomes effective in a position of responsibility, as a supportive and available network of dependable others is necessary to properly and consistently discharge one's responsibilities, be they those of corporate executive, professional, laborer, salesman, or parent. Attachment style has a fundamental impact upon one's ability to establish healthy interdependencies with others.

Interdependency is a more realistic way to characterize effective relationships at any level of development. In the extreme example, while we might see the newborn as utterly and completely dependent and mother as totally giving in their relationship, in fact we are learning more by the day in scientific observations that even the newborn infant is very active in giving off signals to Mom—signals that are critically important for guiding Mom's caregiving. In fact, some theoretical neuroscientists suggest that at birth babies already possess a network of brain cells that guides them to perform "attachment behaviors" toward Mom, just like they have different brain cell networks that guide them to suckle or to turn their heads in response to noise. Mom learns to "read" or interpret each behavior and to respond to the need causing or driving the behavior. Interdependency is the key to successful relationships from the very beginning!

Under ideal circumstances, Mom enters into this new relationship under comfortable social and economic circumstances: with a supportive and capable spouse and family; with a positive and elaborate set of memories of herself being parented as a child; with good mental and physical health; with the pregnancy being timely, welcomed by all, and free of unusual stress; and with positive feelings and fantasies about the new life growing in her womb. By the time of birth, the stage for beginning the attachment is well under way. Experiments show that the newborn infant remembers the sound of his mom's voice, as he would have heard it through the fluid medium of the womb! So not only has Mom already gotten to know him—he's already gotten to know *her*! Interdependency!

Again, under ideal circumstances, the baby has a wonderful set of genes encoding for a healthy body and brain and a delightful temperament; a placid womb experience, complete with a constant array of nutrients in copious supply; total freedom from any infusion of toxins, harmful drugs, or elevated stress hormones from the mother via the umbilical cord; and a smooth birth experience.

The mother-infant pair then get off to a good start, Mom tuning in to baby's signals intensely and consistently enough that she quickly becomes an expert at meeting baby's needs and restoring baby to a comfortable state. By three months of age baby has already begun to learn some tricks of *self-soothing*. As the rest of the first year of life unfolds, baby becomes increasingly aware of Mom as one who provides reliable and effective practical and emotional support. It is not that Mom is always there right on time to meet baby's needs, but instead the mothering is good enough that the two always "make up" quickly after those inevitable occasions when Mom does not quite meet baby's expectations. Researchers would say that the twosome become good at "restoration and repair." (In fact, without these times of "just enough" heightened frustration, baby would not learn the all-important art of "frustration tolerance.")

But what if circumstances during baby's first year of life are not "good enough"? Baby's attachment style is likely to suffer. Under conditions of physical or emotional abuse directly to baby, she is not likely to imbed in her brain an experience of Mom as an available, reliable, and soothing caregiver, even if Mom is not directly at fault. Thus, not only will she bear into later life unconscious memories of the abuse or neglect, but just as sadly, she will most likely develop a seriously impaired attachment style. Chaotic home environments, such as those fraught with violence or the random coming and going of frightening persons, can have a profound adverse effect on infants, even if they are not directly abused. Also, research is suggesting that simply having too many caregivers during the first year or so of life is a risk factor for disturbed attachment capacity, even if the infant is otherwise not exposed to abuse or neglect.

Finally, emotionally neglected babies are likely to develop severe attachment problems even if their physical care is adequate.

IMPLICATIONS FOR ADOPTION

How do these insights from attachment theory and early child development aid parents who are considering adoption? The following guidelines are directly informed by attachment theory. They are offered with the assumption that those parents thoroughly informed regarding the genetic and attachment histories of their adoptive child are best prepared to enjoy a successful parenting experience.

1. Know as much as possible about the genetic history of the child. While no serious mental illness is inherited with nearly 100 percent certainty, we know that children of birth parents with such chronic and severe mental illnesses as schizophrenia and bipolar disorder are at greater risk for developing the disorders themselves than are children of parents without the disorder. Therefore, a consultation with a pediatrician, geneticist, child psychiatrist, or psychologist is wise if the birth parents' history includes serious mental illness.

2. Know as much as possible about the early life of the child. Try to obtain as much of the following information as possible:
   - If the child was raised until the time of adoption by the birth parents, how effective were the parents at meeting the emotional and practical needs of the child?
   - Was the child physically or emotionally abused? If so, was the abuse limited or continuous (and thereby part of the child's regular experience)? Did the abuse occur prior to age two, so that the child would later have far greater difficulty in healing from memories not accessible to consciousness?
   - Was the child neglected? This might be one of the most difficult questions to answer. Many babies fostered from birth by foster parents or orphanages are given good practical care but do not experience a warm, well-attuned bond with a primary caregiver. Such babies are therefore at risk for developing an impaired capacity for attachment to subsequent caregivers.

- How many primary caregivers did the child have in the first eighteen months of life? Although research currently provides limited information regarding the maximum number of primary caregivers tolerable to a baby, the current consensus is that if that number exceeds three, the risk goes up for attachment problems. Such babies may be particularly vulnerable to indiscriminate sociability with strangers later on, while not attaching to the adoptive parents deeply enough.

3. Consider the age and developmental level of the child. Current research suggests that babies adopted prior to about four months of age are unlikely to have formed an attachment style and therefore—all other things being equal—are more likely to form an attachment style that resonates with the attachment style of the adoptive parents (that is, their "state of mind with regard to attachment," as described above.)

4. Reflect on your own history of attachments. What are your memories of attachments to your parents? What have your attachments to others been like throughout adult life? The success of adoptive parents, as with all parents, hinges greatly on their "state of mind with regard to attachment," which in turn is heavily influenced by their conscious and unconscious collection of memories of being parented as children. All potential adoptive parents deserve the opportunity to become thoroughly acquainted with their state of mind with regard to attachment. A good adult psychotherapist familiar with basic attachment theory should prove to be very helpful in this regard. While a course of pre-adoption counseling or therapy would be very helpful for all potential adoptive parents, those with a history of difficult childhood relationships with their parents or difficulty with intimacy in adult relationships would find that effort particularly enlightening and rewarding. The benefit for a smoother, more meaningful, and more successful adoptive experience would make the modest investment in time and money exceedingly rewarding.

5. Remember that you are not the only caregiver to whom your adoptive child may attach. Supposing you assess yourself to have an attachment state of mind other than the autonomous/secure

style as described above. Should you therefore rule yourself out as a potential adoptive parent? Certainly not, although it does mean that you face a more difficult challenge in forming a healthy working relationship with your adoptive child. But you have at least two significant sources of help: a good therapist, as noted above, and other significant caregivers. Remember that a child can develop different attachment styles to different caregivers. Even if you are a single parent (which inevitably renders your parenting challenge even more difficult), you should have access to family and friends, among whom one or more persons may emerge as significant and regular caregivers for your adopted child. No matter how autonomous/secure your own attachment style, you would bless your child were you to invite into her young life one or two other persons with a long history of secure relationships.

6. Be prepared for the most challenging adventure of a lifetime. Even with the most painstaking research and preparation, adoptive parents are likely to face some daunting parenting challenges. At the very least, they are far more likely to receive children with an impaired capacity for healthy attachment. However, we know that with steadfast, unwavering devotion by parents, understanding and support of family and friends, and sometimes expert professional help, even severely attachment-disordered adopted children can develop more secure attachment styles and therefore become happier people.

7. International adoption may entail additional complications regarding attachment. It appears that the principles of attachment during the first year of life are quite universal. Nevertheless, two features of international adoption bear particular notice: (1) If the adoption is of a child thus far exposed to a language other than that of the adoptive parents, a healthy bond may be more difficult to establish. This would seem more likely for children already communicating verbally at the time of adoption. On the other hand, adoptive parents who take the time to learn basic important words in the child's native language can minimize this risk. (2) Significant differences in physical appearance, such as

skin color and facial configuration, may also complicate the identification of parents and adopted child with each other.

A good understanding of the basic principles of attachment theory can be of great value to potential adoptive parents, as well as to their supportive families, friends, and professional support team. Available information regarding the caregiving environment of the child prior to adoption can yield important assumptions regarding the attachment style of the child as she faces the task of forming a solid bond with her new parents. Adoptive parents can further prepare themselves for the adoption by understanding the impact of their own childhood experiences upon their approach to their adopted child.

While impaired attachment capacities can affect both adopted child and adoptive parent, the plasticity of the human brain allows for significant evolution into a more secure attachment style on the part of both. Sometimes ongoing professional help eventually becomes necessary. However, ultimately the single most important factor in a successful adoption is the resolve of the adoptive parents to love their child unconditionally and to maintain a hopeful "whatever it takes" attitude toward removing any and all barriers to a mutually loving and joyful relationship.

3

WHAT DOES HEALTHY ATTACHMENT LOOK, SOUND, AND FEEL LIKE?

You are ready to adopt your new baby, to bring her into the circle of your love and family. You prepare your nest to receive your little one; you make legal and financial preparations and last-minute arrangements with family and friends who will help everything go perfectly. You travel to your child's country and, with both excitement and trepidation, take the long ride to the place where your baby has been living until you arrive to claim her as your own.

On entering the building, you hear a crying baby and know instantly that this child is yours: the baby you have known in your heart and who has longed for you since the day she was conceived.

A caregiver brings to you a baby girl, howling with a red face and wrapped in a blanket, waiting to be loved as only you can love her. She is handed to you. Surprised, she stops crying, looks into your eyes, takes a measure of who you are and why you are there, and just as it is in the movies and fairy tales, she melts into your arms, never to be upset, scared, or lonely again.

This is the ideal of healthy attachment that we would all love to see every time a baby is placed in the arms of her "Forever Parents," the people who want so much to create a life of happiness, fulfillment, and health for her.

There is a famous painting by Mary Cassatt in which a child and mother are gazing into each other's eyes, the child's pudgy hand gently caressing her mother's cheek as the mother calmly and lovingly holds her child safely in her love. What does strong, healthy, calm attachment look like? For me, this particular picture by Cassatt says it all. I keep a print in my office to remind me, and the families I work with, of this representation of our goal.

ATTACHMENT IN THE ANIMAL KINGDOM

Animals in nature also can serve as a model of what healthy attachment looks like. They remind us of the picture of how nature meant for off-spring to be cared for. We humans may have a bigger "thinking" brain than other mammals, but we surely don't have any more "attachment smarts" than the other animal mothers and fathers. How do they learn what is so healthy? And how is it that we humans seem to have forgot-ten, or refuse to accept the importance of consistently performing so many critically necessary attaching behaviors?

These questions stem from the running conflict over what dictates our behavior: genetics versus environment, or nature versus nurture. We are born with the instinct to parent, and as long as that instinct is reinforced, it is with us when we need it. By being nurtured and well cared for by loving parents, our instincts are strengthened and, without major or traumatic interruptions, we ourselves develop into good parents.

However, if that instinct is not reinforced, or if it is confused by mixed signals (for example, if words like "I love you and I will take care of you" are mixed with behaviors that demonstrate the opposite, such as abuse or neglect), then the instinct is damaged.

Observe baby ducklings, for instance. We've all seen how those adorable baby ducklings, immediately after they are born, follow their mother in a straight line. The need to fall into almost a military-type line and follow is not something they think about, but something they simply do, as a matter of instinct.

Studies have shown that if a duckling is kept from following that instinct, that inborn understanding and urge to follow Mom in a line, the instinct becomes damaged and actually lost. The duckling must now be taught, in another, different area of the brain, to follow. It is no longer an instinct, but rather becomes a learned behavior. In other words, in studying the duckling's brain in action, a different part of the brain "lights up" when a duckling naturally, instinctively follows Mother duck than when the duckling loses its instinctive way of following and now has to learn to follow. I assign families the homework of watching nature shows on television, of putting up pictures of healthy animal attachment, and of discussing how nature meant for us to care for our young. Look carefully at the examples in nature around us, for we can easily learn what instinct tells us about healthy attachment.

As an example, I like a video entitled *Nature's Babies: Animal Families* (see the references at the end of the book for information on this). This six-hour video is split into ten-minute segments, each featuring a different animal—from pigs to praying mantises! It highlights how mothers throughout the animal kingdom nurture and protect their young ones.

The fascinating and instructive research begun by psychologist Harry Harlow—the famous "monkey studies"—suggests to us how much animals other than humans have to teach us about instinct-driven attachment needs, and the strength of either reinforcing or interrupting that drive.

These examples are oversimplifications of a complicated process of bonding and attachment, but they highlight the fact that we do have illustrations in nature and scientific research to give us insights into what is healthy—what nature intended for our little ones.

ATTACHMENT IN NEWBORNS

To outsiders, babies' cries and protests may sound the same. A mother once told me that the day after her son was born, she heard him crying from the nursery at the other end of the long hospital hallway. She told the nurse that her son was crying and asked why no one was picking him up. The nurse replied, "You can't possibly tell that's your baby! They all sound pretty much alike." An hour later the nurse returned to apologize to the mother, saying that yes, it had been her son crying. The doctor had in fact been performing a routine medical procedure at the time and that baby did *not* like it and *definitely* wanted his mommy!

How does a mother know her own baby? That's part of nature's bonding process. And how does she differentiate what her baby's cries mean? That's part of the instinct of attunement and parent-child communication, too.

It was fascinating for me to learn about how closely attuned a mother and child can be from the observations of a friend who worked as a physician in a bush hospital in Tanzania. He told of the privilege he had of getting to know a young pregnant woman who farmed in the fields with her family and community members. As she worked, the woman cradled her one-year-old daughter across her chest in a colorful cloth wrap. During early labor with her second pregnancy, the woman continued to work in the field. When labor advanced, elders helped her to the side of the field, where the one-year-old girl was cared for by her grandmother. The pregnant woman soon squatted in a position that allowed gravity to ease the birth. When the new baby was born, the mother cleaned him off with the cradling cloth, then positioned him inside it, keeping him against her skin and within easy reach of her nipple. This new mother of two rested for a while and then resumed her work in the field.

This is not an unusual story in many parts of the world. Women who are physically able have often delivered babies in the course of their work and spent only a few hours recovering before returning to their usual tasks. What I think is remarkable about this story is the connection that this mother has with her children, and I understand this is not in any way unique in her culture. In this story the one-year-old daughter moves from living in the cradle wrap on her mother's chest to being carried regularly on her mother's back. The new son takes the daughter's previous place in the wrap on Mom's chest. This mother can tell from her babies' wriggling when they need to urinate or defecate. She holds them away from her body, allows them to void, and then returns them to the safest of all places, firmly held against her body. Talk about being so in tune with your baby that you know *before* he or she needs to go to the bathroom! As one mother said to me, "Boy, think of what that would do to avoid diaper rash!"

Phyllis Booth, clinical director at the Theraplay Institute in Wilmette, Illinois, says this about adding a child into the "attunement circle" of a family:

> Parenting a lively, responsive infant is richly rewarding and can be full of warmth, excitement, and joy. The feeding that calms a frantic infant into a state of blissful sleep, the play that brings the first belly laugh, the attuned interaction that engages a fretful child, the eye contact, touch, and physical play that leads to the capacity to self-regulate: these are the experiences that create secure attachments and that all parents look forward to when they anticipate bringing a new child into their family. (Booth 2002)

These bonding activities are all part of the first-year attachment cycle discussed earlier—a cycle that is repeated time after time in the average life of an infant with an attentive and loving caregiver. During this period of rapid brain development, the infant is learning that "the world, as represented by Mom, is a safe place for me to be. Therefore, I can spend all of the appropriate and necessary energy that is required to make sure that my brain and body can develop the way they're supposed to. I don't have to waste precious energy being afraid and being worried that I won't be fed, kept warm, prote:ted from predators, and loved as nature meant for me to be." This is the very picture of healthy attachment.

THE NEED FOR SAFETY

ATTACh, the Association for Treatment and Training in the Attachment of Children, defines attachment as follows: "Attachment is a reciprocal process by which an emotional connection develops between an infant and his/her primary caregiver. It influences the child's physical, neurological, cognitive and psychological development. It becomes the basis for development of basic trust or mistrust, and shapes how the child will relate to the world, learn, and form relationships throughout life." Conversely, researcher and practitioner Bruce Perry, M.D., Ph.D., and founder of the Child Trauma Academy writes this of "the threatened child":

> When we are under threat, our minds and bodies will respond in an adaptive fashion, making changes in our state of arousal (mental state), our style of thinking (cognition) and in our body's physiology (e.g., increased heart rate, muscle tone, rate of respiration). . . . The more threatened we become, the more "primitive" (or regressed) our style of thinking and behaving becomes. When a traumatized child is in a state of alarm, . . . they will be less capable of concentrating, they will be more anxious and they will pay more attention to "non-verbal" cues such as tone of voice, body posture and facial expressions. This has important implications for understanding the way the child is processing, learning and reacting in a given situation. (Perry 2001)

Babies need a place where they feel safe and cared for. They need a relationship in which they can be totally relaxed and know, down to their bones and the depth of their souls, that they will be kept safe from harm.

Can we guarantee this to our children? No, of course not. But they need to believe it. They need to believe that we are "Superwoman" and "Superman." Look at our most beloved fairy tales, such as Cinderella, Snow White, Hansel and Gretel, and other classics. The "good guys" always win in the end. You will not find beloved fairy tales in which the "bad guys" win. Children need to believe that they are safe, that the adults in their lives are invincible, and that, by extension, the world is a secure and happy place (Bettelheim 1989).

Why is "And they all lived happily ever after" one of the most common and popular endings for a fairy tale? According to Bettelheim, it is mainly because children cannot yet handle the uncertainties of life. It's too early for them to know that sometimes the "bad guy" is the one who seems to live happily ever after and the "good guy" sometimes ends up rolling down the hill to the sea in a spiked barrel.

When our children are afraid to go on the merry-go-round for the first time, what do we say as parents? We say, "You'll be fine, I'm sure. You're just worried because it's your first time. I was, too. But it's okay. You'll love it—really!"

Do we truly know it will be a safe experience and that they'll love it? No, of course not. We say these things so our children will have the confidence to try new things. We want them to know that we have been there, too, and we want them to know what our experience was, what the outcome was, and that they can trust us to guide them.

Joe Kelly, the author of a wonderful series of articles about attachment in "Families with Children from China," writes that if the infant's needs for food, warmth, and comfort are met, if Mom and Dad are there for him, "the child learns that the world is a good place, one worthy of his trust. Knowing that the world is a place to be trusted is what gives the child the confidence to learn and explore and tolerate the frustrations that are an inevitable part of growth and independence" (Kelly 2002). In contrast, "a child who is abused, abandoned, kept in an institutional setting, moved around a lot, etc., does not see the world as a place to be trusted. This child becomes hypersensitive: even the slightest frustration becomes a reminder of the rejection experienced as an infant."

SAFETY AND NEUROLOGY

Even given our limited understanding of neurology and child development, there is no doubt that there is a neurological basis for attachment. Feeling safe has a positive effect on the nervous system, and it allows the baby's nervous system to carry out its main job, that of completing healthy development. Conversely, fear produces chemical changes in our nervous system. If a baby's tender, developing brain is exposed to increased levels of these fear and anxiety chemicals too often or over too long a period, the brain itself, although otherwise healthy functioning, can become seriously damaged.

At birth, the various systems of the brain naturally allow us to use our parents' care to learn how to "self-regulate." As babies we become agitated (hungry, afraid, and excited) and ask for help to calm down (to be fed, to be kept safe, and relax or be soothed). As infants, we can cry when we're wet or hungry or to let someone know we're frightened or unhappy. The rising state of agitation is met over and over again by our guides who return us to a place of safety, a state of knowing that we are important, that we are special and that we are safe and in loving hands. Our brains, too, learn the rhythm of becoming agitated and then calming.

But when we are not fed or when we are left in a state of fear or unhappiness, we learn two things: that this unhappy state must be the natural state of affairs (i.e., that the world is not a safe place) and that "I am not the most favored child in the universe" (i.e., that I must be basically unlovable). Many of the children I meet in my practice believe deep down in their very core of self-concept that they must be bad or they would not have somehow brought upon themselves the abuse or neglect that they suffered.

If fear becomes a natural state, we adapt to this state of *hyperarousal* by resetting our baseline. In research studies, babies who live in a constant state of fear have been found to have dramatically higher levels of cortisol, a stress hormone, than most babies. If we believe we are not meant to receive love, nurture, and protection, we give up. If a baby's cries are ignored long enough, he will stop wasting energy and will not expect things to change. For further learning about this, look to John Bowlby, the founder of attachment theory, who has written an excellent description of the state of despair in which these neglected babies live. "Attachment research clearly demonstrates that communication between caregiver and infant shapes the way in which the child's developing mind learns to process information" (quoted in Siegel 1999).

Perhaps I can illustrate this concept of resetting one's baseline by using the situation of a city dweller who becomes accustomed to the constant noise of traffic, sirens, car alarms, thumping car radios, and rumbling trains or subways. After a while, it becomes simply background noise to him, part of his life. In fact, if he goes on vacation to a quiet spot in the country, he may actually have trouble sleeping because his brain is so used to this noise. Something's missing in the peace of the mountains or the quiet of the countryside, and it may take him a while to adjust to this new environment.

HOW DO I KNOW WHAT'S NORMAL?

Something I hear very often is a parent's lament that he or she did not bring the child in earlier for an evaluation. This almost always takes one of two forms: "I didn't know what normal was" or "Everyone said our baby would be just fine in time, if only we would . . ."

The first version of the lament often comes from first-time parents (of birth or adopted children). Obviously, we don't cognitively remember much of our infancy, so how can we know if what we're seeing in our little one is what we experienced ourselves? In most cases, having had younger siblings doesn't help much, either: we were probably too busy with our own development at the time to notice much about what a younger brother or sister was doing or how our parents were handling that moment's parenting task.

Memories from those early years, too, are notoriously poor: Did our baby brother cut his front teeth on the bottom before he said "Mama" or after? Was little sister still drinking out of her bottle and carrying her teddy bear when she went to nursery school, or had she given them up?

Give yourself a break! It's not so important to remember these things because we have at our disposal a plethora of resources to describe, define, and categorize "normal" for us. I do not believe there is an absolute "normal," but there is a range of what we expect to see happening in a young one's life at various ages and stages.

As Dr. John Biever wrote in chapter 2, Mary Ainsworth is a well-known expert in infant and child attachment who studied with John Bowlby and took his work several steps further in our understanding of healthy and unhealthy attachment. Ainsworth (1978) found the following attachment behaviors in children throughout the world. The child

1. Follows the primary caregivers
2. Engages in reciprocal interactions with the primary caregivers
3. Interacts gently with the primary caregivers
4. Refuses comfort from anyone except the primary caregivers
5. Engages in long-lasting and intense eye contact with the primary caregivers
6. Protests violently and for long periods when the primary caregivers are absent
7. Complies with the primary caregivers' requests, even when they are at odds with what the child wants.

Whatever your spiritual, religious, philosophical views, we all agree, I'm sure, that there does seem to be a more or less "natural order" to things—a way in which nature seems to want life to happen. This "natural order" is used to help us make sense of our health and everyday lives. For example, when we go to the doctor's office to have our blood levels checked for abnormalities, each category being measured has a range that is considered "within normal limits" (doctors even have an acronym for it: WNL). If there were no "normal" or acceptable ranges, we would not be looking at people who compulsively lie, steal, or hurt others, for example, as being "abnormal."

I realize that talking about what is "normal" is not very politically correct in this day and age. However, I am talking here about "normal" as being what people throughout history, and across various domains and fields of study, have called healthy, acceptable, expected, or otherwise just plain "okay" behavior—behavior that constitutes the loving, close relationship we will use as our model of healthy attachment.

If you're concerned about "what is normal," my advice is to find a book, video, or website about child development (*not* a chat room or parent-generated list) that you like and with which you feel comfortable. Make sure your resources

- Are written by professionals with good experience and credentials
- Are written in a style you like and find easy to read
- Are put together with the kind of format you are comfortable using; for example, if you are a "chart person," look for a resource that puts the information in that format
- Include good resource lists of their own, in case there is something you wish to look up in further detail
- Give you enough supportive information to help you feel good about your parenting

The second type of lament comes from listening to ill-informed or judgmental, albeit well-meaning friends or family members: perhaps something like, "Your baby is just fine and simply needs more love." This is confusing and often misleading. Remember that *you* are the best expert on your child—not a grandparent, your child's nursery school teacher, or even necessarily a mental health professional. Anyone who wants to help you must accept that *you* know your child better than anyone. After all, you treasured this child in your heart long before laying eyes on her and long before anyone else in your family met her. You are the one who sleeps with her, feeds her, knows her heartbeat and the meaning of each babble and cry. Take and maintain your place as the most important person in your child's life. If you are insecure about that place, your child will be insecure about trusting you to know what is best for her. Trust yourself.

4

HEALTHY ATTACHMENT
INTERRUPTED

We had a dream that everything would be perfect. Here we were swooping in and rescuing this little boy from an orphanage, and of course he would be so grateful that he would love us automatically. But as we learned about attachment disorder, we had to let go of that dream and realize that wasn't how it was going to be.

—MOTHER OF AN ADOPTED RUSSIAN BOY

It's a grieving process. Your expectations must change; you don't want to lose the dream, but you have to. This child may never have any semblance of a normal happy life, and that's from something that happened to him in his first years of life. That damage has been enough to shape his future. It's a very horrifying thing. He'll never have anything like I'd want for him. Those hopes are gone, sadly enough.

—MOTHER OF AN ADOPTED ROMANIAN BOY

This chapter is one of those I would classify as "hard to take": it deals with sad emotions and experiences nobody wants to believe could happen to them. Please understand: we know that many, indeed most, adoptions are happy and healthy. We know many families that are made whole through the wonder of adoption. Many, *most*, "families by choice," as some people call adoptive families, are well functioning and healthy, and adopted children are smoothly integrated into a loving, safe family environment in which they thrive.

But not all children are so lucky: "Mental health experts agree that more children with some sort of emotional or psychiatric disturbance are surfacing in the offices of psychiatrists and psychologists and in hospital emergency rooms. A disturbing report issued by the U.S. Surgeon General's office in 1999 reveals that 12 million children in this country between the ages of 9 and 17—or 20 percent—have a diagnosable psychiatric disorder" (Hochman 2003). Many of the children included in the surgeon general's report, those suffering with long-standing emotional pain and severe behavioral and psychological and learning problems, are children who have developed significant attachment problems or are living with the long-term effects of significant emotional trauma.

We hope that the information presented in this book will show you what you need to understand and practice to maximize the chances of securing the best, most healthy, happy, loving attachment. You are going to hear about what can happen when normal, healthy attachment, with its commensurate neurological development, is interrupted. For the sake of the children and families who were not well prepared, through no fault of their own, to form a loving, trusting, healthy attachment, we will look at the excruciating possibilities that can occur when damage happens at an early age and repairs are not made early and thoroughly.

So, as uncomfortable as it is, I need for you to imagine the unthinkable. Imagine that your beautiful, long-awaited little one is placed in your arms, red and pinched from crying or howling, or worse, lying inert and looking at the ceiling, appearing to see little or nothing of the world around him. You are sure that with time and enough love, the fear or apathy will melt, and the dreaded "failure-to-thrive" look on his otherwise perfect little face will be replaced with joy to match your own. And so, with tears of happiness and anticipation, you receive into your arms, heart, and family this fragile creature who is now totally dependent on adults he has never met and has no reason to believe will care for him any better than he has been treated previously.

You look into his eyes. You want so desperately for him to look back, to relax and smile, for all his hurts and past fears to ease out of his body, into yours if that's what it takes. You are willing and ready—even eager— to absorb the pain he has experienced so he can now be free to open his heart to you, to your love and joy at being his Forever Mother or Forever Father.

Sadly, he doesn't stop crying. He doesn't "melt." His pain is still very visible on his face and in the tension in his body or his utter lack of responsiveness. What's wrong? Why doesn't he feel the intensity of your wanting—*willing*—him to be happy, relaxed, safe, *loved*?

WHAT ATTACHMENT DISORDER IS AND WHY IT HAPPENS

It's difficult to imagine that just a loving gaze into your baby's eyes could cause him to become so uncomfortable that the hormones of self-defense, literally of survival, would shoot up to an extremely high intensity. But that is what happens to children with reactive attachment disorder and other significant attachment issues.

Your young one was born into the world ready to trust adults, namely and foremost his mother, father, immediate family, or primary caregiver. "Trust us," they said, by the very nature of bearing a child and bringing that child into the world. "We will keep you safe; that's our job." Again by nature, the baby says, "Okay, that's your job. I'll do mine, which is to trust." But instead of being rewarded with the kind of nuturing babies by nature expect, some children's trust is betrayed.

Broken Trust: Neglect

What do some babies actually experience? Perhaps being "cared for" by family members who are abusive, impatient, and grossly inept. Perhaps being thrust into an institution where there is only enough attention to keep the baby alive. Perhaps becoming a "pass-around baby" without knowing which form of abuse, neglect, or just plain inattention to expect, and from whom, from one day to the next.

In any of these instances the child's innately trusting nature can be badly damaged. At the very least, being removed from the birth mother is enough to cause some children to become terrified and lose faith that the world is a safe place. Remember, some of these children were born to women who abused alcohol or drugs during pregnancy, were depressed or highly anxious, or experienced other situations during pregnancy, such as being in an abusive situation themselves, that might have predisposed the baby to be emotionally or neurologically fragile. As infants, these young ones may already have neurological difficulties. Once that primal trust is broken, the internal world of the infant is fear, confusion, distress, and turmoil.

This reaction isn't a choice on the child's part, even when he is older and capable of cognitive thought. The reactions themselves become programmed into the child's brain and part of his intrinsic neurological makeup. This is why the more common child therapies such as behavior modification, traditional family therapy, and play therapy are not very effective for children with attachment issues. In the earliest, most active stages of development, the child's brain stops developing in the natural, healthy model. The child has become "stuck" in the *hypervigilant* mode of believing what he has found to be the truth: "I'm not safe in the world. The world is scary. Ultimately, no one out there can take care of me. I can depend only on me." In the worst of situations, the infant slides into what the father of attachment, John Bowlby, calls the "despair state" and literally stops caring about survival at all.

Once a bit older, the "fight or flight" child is so primed for a fight that almost any action on the part of a parent, no matter how innocent (e.g., suggesting what clothes to wear), is perceived as a challenge and a threat and becomes a trigger for *hyperreactive* behavior. The child's brain bypasses reasoning and cognitive decision making and reverts to the behavior that, after all, allowed him to survive his difficult early months and years.

Without help, these children can spend years, or even their whole lives, in *"fight, flight, or freeze"* mode. They learned early on that if they don't have control, they are in jeopardy. They are hypervigilant, always scanning, trying desperately to be ready for the next attack—even though they "know" in at least one part of their brain that there is no rational reason to expect such an attack. After adoption they have had the constant experience of being with safe and loving parents. But their rational brain doesn't "talk" to the rest of the brain because this is not where they process information about safety. They want and need to relax and trust others. But their brains have been formed to react in a way that makes it impossible for them to do just that.

Because the child with serious attachment problems has spent so much energy protecting himself in early life or often has not received adequate or appropriate stimulation, he is more than likely "out of sync" with his chronological age. I will repeat throughout the book that parents should always pay attention to their child's emotional age and behavior, not the way he "should" be acting based on his chronological age. A child with attachment issues cannot be expected to fit into standard development charts, at least not until significant healing has happened.

Trauma

Trauma is another potential cause of attachment disorder. Trauma is a painful emotional experience or shock that can create substantial and often long-lasting damage to the psychological development and well-being of the individual. *Traumatic events* are exceptional situations of helplessness and distress that a person experiences firsthand, observes, or learns about that might jeopardize the physical or psychological integrity of the individual or those close to him or her. Some traumatic events for children include

- Abandonment/loss of family
- Neglect
- Physical abuse
- Emotional abuse
- Sexual abuse
- Extreme parental stress
- Parental mental illness, including parental substance abuse
- Extreme poverty

- Physical illness, including malnutrition and physical problems such as recurring ear infections or other painful medical conditions
- Divorce between primary caregivers
- Inadequate group care/out-of-home care

Recent research has shown that when an event is perceived to be traumatic or life threatening, part of the brain that gives language to the experience stops working. Instead, the traumatic event gets stored in the sensory-motor domain of the brain. Like all memory, traumatic memory gets stored too. To people who have experienced trauma, perfectly normal and otherwise benign situations can be perceived to carry some hidden threat, as in the following account by the mother of a five-year-old girl adopted from China:

> Wednesday morning I had to take one of the cats to the vet. Shelley had to come (no school this week), which was very unfortunate. The smell of the vet's office causes what my husband and I believe to be post-traumatic stress disorder—it smells like the hospital we had to take her to in China. She was very agitated the whole time and went into her nonsense chatter mode for nearly an hour. It's a repeated six-syllable rhythmic pattern, which she says over and over with little variation. I had a very hard time getting her to stop, partly because I could not hold her since I had to hold the cat and talk to the vet at the same time. Very upsetting. It had been a long time since we had been to the vet, and Shelley and I had both forgotten how hard it was for her. But when we got home I held her and I also tried to explain to her why I thought she was scared when we went to the vet. It seemed to help. The next day *she* had to go to the doctor. Ugh!

When people respond to their environment out of fear of a potential threat, they become hypervigilant, their heart rate is often higher than normal, even when they are resting, and their adrenaline system is always pumped up, ready for "fight, flight, or freeze." This "fight, flight, or freeze" phenomenon is evident in children who often appear to be defensive, who are ready to blame others, who need to control every situation they encounter, who are ready to fight back when there is nothing to fight about, or who seem to "check out" and become nonresponsive to many requests.

For a much more in-depth explanation of brain development and function relative to early emotional trauma, read Daniel Siegel's extraordinary and thorough work titled *The Developing Mind* (1999). Here is a passage from his introduction that gives at least the beginning of the complex-yet-simple explanation of how early trauma can "set up" the brain for later dysfunction:

> Though experience shapes the activity of the brain and the strength of neuronal connections throughout life, experience early in life may be especially crucial in organizing the way the basic structures of the brain develop. For example, traumatic experiences at the beginning of life may have more profound effects on the "deeper" structures of the brain, which are responsible for basic regulatory capacities and enable the mind to respond later to stress. Thus we see that abused children have elevated baseline and reactive stress hormone levels....Early in life, interpersonal relationships are a primary source of the experience that shapes how genes express themselves within the brain. (pp. 13-14)

WHY CHILDREN HAVE DIFFICULTIES COPING WITH NEGLECT AND TRAUMA

Attachment disorder has some similarities to post-traumatic stress disorder—the syndrome that may occur, for instance, with soldiers who have witnessed horrific scenes in battle, or with people who have been sexually assaulted. But even our soldiers are at least eighteen years old; they have had that long to learn how to cope with most of life's problems, even if these episodes have not been on the scale of a battlefield.

Babies who are abused or neglected, on the other hand, do not have even that short experience with life and problem solving; they have absolutely no experience on which they can rely and have extremely limited resources to care for themselves in traumatic situations. Babies cannot dial 911, run for help, or fight back. They are, in effect, almost helpless in the face of traumatic events, including neglect.

How an Adult Reacts

Trust is the basis on which healthy attachment develops. So let's look at an example of us, as adults, regarding trust. Then we will relate it—similarities and differences—to infants and young children.

Pretend you are sitting in a lecture hall listening to a speaker discussing a topic of great importance to you. The lights are low and the room is large and filled with a hundred people you don't know, including the people sitting on either side of you. You have made a decision, probably without much conscious thought, to allow yourself to be physically very close to these two people you don't know, because your motivation is high—you want to hear the speaker and this was the seating arrangement available—and your past experience is that in most cases sitting next to people you don't know in this type of a setting is perfectly safe.

So there you are trusting the situation to be a safe, positive one, sitting, listening, and looking toward the front of the room, and attending in a state that attachment and bonding psychiatrist Martha Welch calls "calm alert" (Welch 1988). In other words, you are paying close attention to the speaker, while the rest of your body is calm enough to allow your energy to support this attentive focus.

In the midst of your rapt attention, from out of nowhere, the person sitting on your right just hauls off and gives you a big roundhouse punch in the face! What in the world could be happening? After the first few moments of stunned disbelief and silence, you look at the person and there he is, sitting calmly watching and listening to the speaker, just as you yourself had been only a few short moments before. There is no indication from that person that he has just done something totally and unacceptably out of the norms of our commonly accepted civilized behaviors.

What do you choose to do? What are your options? On what do you base your reactions?

As a mature adult, with years of life experience and many resources available to you, you have a variety of options. You may choose to act in a more-or-less cognitive fashion: recalling all of your learning and understanding of human behavior, you may think about what could have been happening to this person that he would do such a thing. You may try cognitively, thoughtwise, to figure out why the person did what he did so you can consciously decide how you want to respond.

You can think through the medical conditions that may have propelled this person into the action. Could the person have Tourette's syndrome? In that case, he may have had little control over the physical act of his arm flying out into the face of the person sitting in the next seat—*your* face. Or, could someone who looks remarkably like you have abused the person in childhood, and the speaker just alluded to something that sent this person reeling back into preverbal, unconscious memory to the time that the abuse occurred? He may not even have been aware of the pent-up anger lashing out in your direction. Or what if the person has a form of epilepsy, or a type of seizure disorder and not only has no control of his physical behavior at some times, but also has little awareness of the actions of his body parts? After your intial reaction, you could then take action: to move away, alert a security guard, call for medical assistance—or all of these things at once!

How a Child Reacts

The above chain of reasoning is all cognitive; it's based on rational thought. But a baby doesn't know what is normal social behavior and certainly does not know about epilepsy and other ailments. Nor does a baby have the physical ability to just move himself out of a dangerous or frightening situation or to "report" problems to appropriate adults.

A baby simply experiences what is given to him or her, and for a high number of adopted children, that involves prenatal or infant abuse or neglect. At the very least, it involves a fairly traumatic "culture shock": losing his birth mom, moving into a new family, a new set of smells, sounds, norms of behavior, foods, style of being cared for, and on and on.

A baby in this situation cannot figure out why he is being neglected or abused or why things are changing so drastically. He doesn't have the ability to process what is happening on any level other than two basic choices: "I can trust this person to keep me safe" or "I'm afraid! I need to protect myself." The baby has no means of deciding if someone's action is a threat to him or not, so to be safe, he perceives everything, instinctively, as a threat. The child has limited ways to negotiate his own safety, except for behaviors that get immediate attention or provide for relief from frustration. Physically, the baby does not have a wide range of behaviors: he can lash out, cover his head, or pretend he is not there if the fear or pain is too intense. We are learning through various medical studies that his physiology changes: his chemistry changes and anxiety levels increase.

If this happens often enough, or if it goes on for long enough, the reaction becomes a pattern: a pattern of neurologically based mistrust. Even when *we* know he is safe, almost anything from the environment can trigger emotional "cues" that make *him* feel threatened.

WHAT RAD LOOKS LIKE: JADE AND MIKE

The American Psychiatric Association describes RAD as follows:

> Reactive Attachment Disorder (RAD) is a complex psychiatric condition that affects a small number of children. It is characterized by problems with the formation of emotional attachments to others that are present before age five. A parent or a physician may first notice problems in attachment with the caregiver that ordinarily forms in the latter part of the first year of the child's life. The child with RAD may appear detached, unresponsive, inhibited or reluctant to engage in age-appropriate social interactions. Alternatively, some children with RAD may be overly and inappropriately social or familiar, even with strangers. The social and emotional problems associated with RAD may persist, as the child grows older. (American Psychiatric Association 2000)

The Association for Treatment and Training in the Attachment of Children defines attachment disorder this way:

> Attachment disorder is a treatable condition in which there is a significant dysfunction in an individual's ability to trust or engage in reciprocal, loving, lasting relationships. An attachment disorder occurs due to traumatic disruption or other interferences with the caregiver-child bond during the first years of life. It can distort future stages of development and impact a person's cognitive, neurological, social and emotional functioning. It may also increase the risk of other serious emotional and behavioral problems. (ATTACh, 2003)

Contrast this with ATTACh's definition of attachment:

Attachment is a reciprocal process by which an emotional connection develops between an infant and his/her primary caregiver. It influences the child's physical, neurological, cognitive and psychological development. It becomes the basis for development of basic trust or mistrust, and shapes how the child will relate to the world, learn, and form relationships throughout life. (ATTACh, 2003).

With these clinical definitions in mind, let's look at how RAD has affected the lives of two particular youngsters.

Jade

Jade was adopted at age four months from Korea, the youngest of five children. Now, in her adoptive Forever Family, she has a younger brother, the birth child of her adoptive parents. Her adoptive parents are loving, caring, non-Asian, and middle-class. I first evaluated Jade when she was thirteen years and ten months old and wrote this as part of her initial evaluation report, based on history by parents and adoption information, previous psychiatric and psychological reports, school records, observation, an interview, and my own evaluation:

Jade has always been aggressive toward other children, including her brother. She has a need to be in control of her peers, is destructive, is jealous of her brother, blames him and others for her behaviors, lies and steals from the family and others. She began shoplifting at age nine and was arrested for this at age eleven. Jade has had severe difficulties dealing with classmates and peers, preying on and stalking other students. She is unable to make friends, primarily because they mistrust her. She has been suspended from school, has run away, has a strained relationship with her parents, is very resistant to structure and is impulsive and anxious, especially in groups, including her family. Jade is both "street smart" and extremely bright.

Because of her severe difficulty interacting with peers, most of her school career has been home schooling by her mother. She attended an institute for intellectually gifted children in the fall of the fourth and fifth grades but needed to finish each year home-schooled. In the fifth grade she attended thirty days at an international school, then again was home-schooled. She was suspended from public school in sixth grade after multiple suspensions for stealing, forging notes supposedly written by parents, and stalking a boy classmate. She has been home-schooled since that time.

Jade has difficulty distinguishing between fantasy and reality. An avid reader, she imagines herself as the characters, claiming the spirits of the characters talk to her. She is very superstitious and interested in the occult. She has made inappropriate contact with strangers on the Internet.

Jade has had traditional psychotherapy by various professionals with minimal success. At age eleven she was diagnosed by a psychiatrist as suffering from cyclothymic disorder and disruptive behavior disorder. Her psychiatrist reports that Jade exhibits symptoms of obsessive-compulsive disorder; conduct disorder, childhood onset type; and post-traumatic stress disorder. Jade reports she feels highly anxious in crowds, needing to "escape" when she is with too many people, and that she experiences stomach upset much of the time. Her mother reports that Jade is easily startled, especially with noises that others experience as normal but that Jade experiences as very loud.

Jade has always been an excellent academic student, testing in the superior range of intelligence. In fact, school testing places her in the ninety-seventh to ninety-ninth percentile of cognitive ability. She is very creative and artistic, excelling at drawing and writing.

Jade's primary diagnosis after evaluation was reactive attachment disorder of infancy or early childhood, disinhibited type, with a secondary diagnosis of post-traumatic stress disorder, chronic type (client evaluation).

As is evident from this profile, Jade exhibits many of the typical features of RAD:

- Lying
- Inability to trust
- Oppositional, acting-out behavior
- Engaging in dangerous behavior
- Apparent desire to keep others at a distance
- Hypervigilance

Later in this book you will learn about the exceptional and reward-ing strides that Jade, an extremely articulate and insightful young woman, has made in her life with the help of her family and intensive therapy.

Mike

Mike was born in Romania in 1989. As a psychiatrist who evaluated him at age ten and a half noted, "Michael's history is significant for early neglect and abandonment by his mother at some point after his first birthday. Nothing is known of his life circumstances until he was placed in foster care for one month prior to his adoption at eighteen months of age." Just before he was adopted, Mike suffered serious burns of the neck, chest, and feet when he was accidentally exposed to boiling water. The wounds became infected and required extensive and painful treat-ment. In addition, at the time of his adoption he was diagnosed with anemia, bronchitis, and malnourishment. By the age of five he had undergone surgery for a hernia repair, eye muscle correction, and removal of his tonsils and adenoids.

Mike was adopted by wonderful, loving people who are extremely structured yet patient with Mike. Mom is a professional who works with children in Mike's school district. I asked Mike's mother to tell me about a typical weekend with him. This is what she described:

On the weekend Mike normally sleeps late because he will often stay up until 1 to 2 a.m. He would stay up even later, but I now insist that he go to bed when we do because of the house damage we have incurred when he is up alone.

In the morning Mike tends to be groggy and will often sit in front of the TV so that Randy [Mike's younger brother, the birth child of this adoptive couple] cannot see. This prompts the first morning confrontation. He often changes the channel, although there is another TV to watch. If we tell him to watch the other TV, he com-plains bitterly that he always is the one who has to go to the other TV; why can't Randy be the one to leave? We used to try to mediate and come to a compromise but have learned after years of frustration that there is no compromise with Mike, and separation tends to be the best way of avoiding multiple fights between the brothers, almost always started by Mike. We have also learned that once things start on the "downward slope," problems escalate, so it is best to put off issues as long as possible.

Mike becomes very engrossed in the TV, PlayStation, and computer. Once he is downstairs it is very hard to get him back upstairs. We often try to get him to eat breakfast immediately after getting up, but he will often sneak downstairs while it is being prepared, and then it is a war to get him to come back up. Multiple requests will have to be made, often with demands that he come up immediately. He will always say, "Wait, wait," but he never comes up, or he will ignore you as if he did not hear you, or angrily yell back at you, throw things and stamp around, but he never comes up willingly or easily. When he does come up, he will have turned the sound of the TV up and will have put on every light and fan in that room before coming up. He will stamp and carry on when asked to go turn things off and will also use that as an excuse to watch TV again.

Once he finally does come up, he will go through cabinets for food that you have already prepared for him, saying he wants something else, knocking things over, leaving the fridge and drawers open, climbing on cabinets and running his hands through other people's food. When he sits down to eat, he will make a tremendous mess throughout the kitchen, getting up repeatedly, walking into other rooms, spilling food and crumbs everywhere, getting out more food even though he has not eaten what is out already and complaining bitterly that he is "not allowed" to eat this or that or do this or that.

He is always belligerent and often picks fights with us or his brother during meals. He will pick on people relentlessly and will "nudge" people until someone loses patience with him. He will talk nonstop in a loud voice, scream for no apparent reason, stand on chairs and spin around the room, knocking into people and things. We often begin breakfast with him downstairs so we can have some peace, then we call him halfway through the meal.

This description was the first of *nine* pages of a weekend as described by Mom and as documented by parents, school, and other professionals, and as observed in therapy with Mike. After reading all pages, I wondered how this family was still functioning at all! Even understanding, as I do, that Mike does not intentionally try to be so disruptive, hurtful, dangerous, and out of control, I marveled at his parents' fortitude in keeping Mike in their home and hearts.

Mike exhibits many of the typical features of RAD:

- Lying
- Hoarding
- Destructive behavior
- Apparent desire to keep others at a distance (refusal to wash, wearing dirty clothes)
- Good behavior when outside the family circle

Mike is one of the few children we treated who, although he did respond in a positive way to attachment therapy and made great strides in self-regulation, did not recover as well as we would have hoped. Despite the best efforts of this persistent family, Mike was eventually admitted to a residential treatment facility for dangerous behavior to allow for more intensive psychiatric intervention than we could offer.

DIAGNOSING RAD

In our specialized practice at the Institute for Children and Families, we see many children and adolescents who are referred to us because they have been diagnosed with RAD or attachment issues or because they have experienced a severe trauma and are not getting better. Or they may come to us because they have a set of behaviors that may be thought to be something else (often attention deficit hyperactivity disorder or oppositional defiant disorder), but the usual therapies haven't helped them get better. Jade, as we saw, had been through several courses of regular child therapy with no success. This was true for Mike as well.

RAD is not a well-known disorder, even among most mental health professionals, physicians, school personnel, and others who work with children and adolescents. Children with serious attachment issues are often misdiagnosed and thus inappropriately treated in therapy and at home, sometimes for years. The result is that they get worse instead of better and often end up in trouble, in jail, or in a psychiatric hospital.

Society is bearing a huge burden by not recognizing and fixing this situation. Misdiagnosis leaves many hearts and lives broken, and these poor children become a huge burden to our families, our schools, our communities, the juvenile justice system, the courts, and the mental health system. A fascinating series of studies around the long-term effects of what is called adverse childhood experiences (ACE) is carefully documenting and tracking what happens to many of the children who are not able to have the benefits of healing from their early abuse or neglect. See Anda et al. (2001, 2002) for more about this issue.

We are becoming increasingly able to diagnose and treat RAD and attachment issues, thanks to the perseverance and insights of dedicated people in the field and current medical research. Some of the evaluation tools we use to diagnose RAD, and various treatments that are proving successful, are discussed in chapter 10.

FOR THOSE INTERESTED IN MORE TECHNICAL INFORMATION

There is quite a bit of medical and other scientific information on attachment available on the Internet and through other resources. If you are interested in more in-depth reading about the neurobiochemical and physiological changes that occur in the developing brain of infants and children with attachment breaks and other traumatic injuries, please consult the references at the end of this book.

As an example of the work that is being done in this field, A. N. Schore, in the February 2002 issue of the *Australia and New Zealand Journal of Psychiatry*, published a fascinating study linking early abuse with the right-brain activities that drive attachment functions. Schore found that "disorganised-disoriented insecure attachment, a pattern common in infants abused in the first two years of life," manifests itself psychologically as "an inability to generate a coherent strategy for coping with relational stress." On a positive note, Schore also found that data suggest "early intervention programs can significantly alter the intergenerational transmission of post-traumatic stress disorders."

ABOUT ANNA

Anna was taken to a Russian orphanage immediately after she was born and stayed there until she was adopted at age twenty months by a single woman with no other children. At age four and a half she began intensive attachment therapy. After less than a year of therapy, she is doing well in kindergarten but retains some self-regulation problems. In the following section, her mother describes some of her experiences with Anna.

On Wednesday we had our first holding time. Anna wanted a bedtime story and I said we should try doing it a new way, alternating sentences while I held her in my lap. She hated this. She was squirming and yelling and kicking.

On Thursday I came downstairs with a power screwdriver and Anna asked if I was going to hurt her. We went straight into holding time.

After I spent a night out without Anna, I sensed a lot of anger from her. She said she was mad at me for not checking on her when I got home. I said that not only did I check on her, I also put her pajama top back on (she frequently takes off her pajama top in the middle of the night; I think it's a test for me). I decided that this was a good time for holding time. I held her and she was very angry.

Anna: Let me go! Let me go! I don't love you!

Mom: You know I can see my reflection in your eyes? Can you see yourself in mine?

Anna: I'm ugly! Don't look at me! I'm a hideous creature!

She squirmed, kicked, and tried to hide her face in my side. I kept kissing her and she kept pushing me away, sometimes so forcefully I thought I'd get a black eye or bloody nose. She screamed, "Don't kiss me! Get your hands off me! You're hurting me!" I kept telling her to do deep breathing. The first breaths were rushed through, but the latter ones in each cycle were slower and better. Once she completely relaxed, I gave her a leg massage. During this time she completely hid her head and sucked her fingers. Holding time lasted forty minutes.

Once we were done, she asked if she could go back to coloring. I went to make some tea for myself and asked if she would like a bottle. She said yes and that she wanted milk in it. We went back to the same place on the sofa and sat in the same position. This time she was completely relaxed. She left me for a minute to get a blanket and a stuffed animal and then came back. When I said, "You're pretty," she said, "You, too." She said that when she told me she didn't love me, she didn't mean it. She drank so much milk we had to go to the store to buy more. I have not seen Anna so relaxed and happy in a very long time.

Bottle time has been happening every day since, at least twice a day. We even bought a new throw blanket just for bottle time.

A few days later, I came into my room carrying a hammer to hang a picture we had just bought. Anna asked if I was going to hurt her, and again we went into holding time.

Anna: Stop! You're hurting me!

Mom: I would never hurt you.

Anna: Yes, you would!

Mom: I love you.

Anna: No, you don't! I don't love you!

At least she was kicking less this time.

On Monday she asked me to help her dress for school (very unusual). When I went into her room, I saw that she took a crayon and colored all over the poster we made of all the ways we are alike. Thankfully I had it framed, so all I have to do is wipe it off. When I brought it to her attention, she asked if I still love her. Why does this feel like a test? It's very frustrating. I wish I could get through to her that I will always love her and will never hurt her. I'm very tired. I feel bad because I can now sense how much she is suffering. I guess I should be happy she is feeling relaxed enough to finally let this stuff out.

ABOUT KEESHA

Keesha is a five-year-old African American girl who was voluntarily placed in foster care twice by the age of fourteen months, both times with the same foster family. She was adopted by this foster family when she was almost five years old. In the following section, her adoptive mother talks about Keesha. She has been in attachment and trauma-reduction therapy for about six months.

Yesterday afternoon Kathy (Keesha's older adopted sister) and Keesha played a couple of games I had for them. They played for quite a while. Eventually they were in the kitchen standing by me, and Keesha sort of spontaneously came up to Kathy and asked if she could hug her. This is very unusual! Kathy kind of backed away and said no. I think I said, "Oh, Kathy!" and she relented, and Keesha hugged her. I'm not sure if Kathy returned the hug or not. She only lets Mark (my husband) and me give her "sideways hugs." But I was so happy that Keesha had that impulse.

Later on in the evening, Keesha drew with a purple marker on the wall in the hallway. I made her try and wash the marks off, but they wouldn't go away. She was worried about what Mark would say. I finally tried bleach and they came off. She said, "Oh, good, now Daddy won't know." But the first thing she did when he came home was take him and show him the place. He just said something like, "Oh, you must not draw on the walls." She came over to me looking very happy, and I said something about how she had told the truth and nothing bad happened.

She danced for us last night. I wish you could see her. She's a hoot. She has a couple of songs she likes, and she "interprets" them. She is soooo dramatic. All of us sat and watched her, and she was in her glory.

Several nights ago she was bugging Kathy relentlessly and I ended up dragging her out of their bedroom. We ended up in the rocking chair with her crying. I said nothing dreadful had happened: Kathy was annoyed and I was annoyed, but I still loved her and nothing she could do would make me stop. She said she could make me stop. I said, "No way!" She said she could knock over the lamp, break the piano, hit me. Of course I said I would still love her. It took quite a while, and lots of rocking, crooning to her, and hugging, but finally she relaxed in my arms, and, I think, began to believe that this love is for real and forever.

II

FOSTERING ATTACHMENT WHEN YOU WELCOME YOUR NEW CHILD

5

Preparing Your Home

You've decided that you really want to adopt. You've thought carefully and realistically about yourself and your family and have decided that you're capable of meeting the challenges that lie ahead. What can you do to start things off on the right foot?

This chapter will describe how to lay the groundwork for attachment. There's a lot you can do before you even meet the new member of your family.

STARTING ATTACHMENT IN YOUR CHILD'S PREADOPTIVE ENVIRONMENT

You can start the attachment process before you even meet your child. A major goal in preparing for adoption is to familiarize the child with what you—his or her new parents—will look, sound, and smell like and also to begin to instill a sense that she or he belongs to you. These actions will begin to create a bond between the child and you, his or her Forever Parents, easing the eventual transition:

- Send some soft, cotton, well-cleaned clothes and toys to the orphanage where your child is waiting, items that will be new and comfortable and that your child will bring with him when he comes home. Work with your adoption agency (or your U.S. liaison in the case of foreign adoption) to ensure that the items actually get to your child.
- Send photos of yourselves to the child. Perhaps you can even make a mobile of the photos.
- Send audiotapes of yourselves speaking or singing to your child.
- Send photos or drawings, perhaps with short descriptions, of your home and neighborhood. Make sure you include pictures and names of pets if there are any.
- Send disposable cameras to the orphanage or social service agency caring for your child. Ask the personnel there to take pictures of your child as she or he grows. Ask them to draw outlines of your child for you.

GETTING YOUR HOUSE READY

There are lots of simple gestures you can make that will help with bonding. On the surface they may not seem necessary, but they can really help. A good example of this is the way you decorate your home.

Many internationally adopted children and some children adopted from here in the United States have compromised immune systems, manifested in such ailments as allergies, asthma, eczema, or seborrhea. They may show what we call neurologic "soft signs" such as hyperreactivity or irritability, which can make the attachment process harder than it may already be. What can you do to help create a healthy, calming atmosphere in your home that will minimize the effect of any potential physical ailments? Here are some suggestions for your family's home environment:

- Use soft, recessed lights or natural lighting, not fluorescents.
- Keep sounds soft. Play soothing music, perhaps from your child's previous environment/country, if it doesn't seem upsetting for your child. Gradually change music to the soothing type you enjoy. (See suggested product list in appendix B for suggestions.)

- Bright colors may be cheerful but may not be best for the baby's sensitive nerves. Pastels or neutrals may be better.
- Avoid volatile organic chemicals (VOCs), which are found in many household products, paints, and furniture. Paints, carpet and carpet glue, and the glue in many pieces of wood furniture can be particularly bad culprits. Most major paint and carpet companies now include at least one line of their products that are specially created as low VOC—seek these out. There isn't a lot of scientific information available yet on the issue of chemical sensitivities and environmental allergies, at least not specifically related to children experiencing early trauma being especially sensitive and hyperreactive. However, there is good anecdotal evidence that using these preventive measures can help, and they certainly can't hurt. There are several companies that market products for allergy-sensitive individuals; a good place to start might be www.gaiam.com, which publishes mail-order catalogs.
- It is critically important that your child be able to navigate in your home (depending on his or her age, of course) without getting into trouble. Childproofing for safety is, of course, essential. But childproofing so your child has as few temptations as possible with which to confirm that he or she is "bad" is also very important. For example, if you don't want your child to eat before dinner, keep food out of the child's reach, rather than constantly having to tell him "No, I already told you not to take that food," and having to use a consequence. Prevention is supremely better than consequencing, and your home is the best place you can childproof so this can happen.

BABY PRODUCTS

Choosing baby products well can also smooth the transition. When you buy clothes, buy soft, already washed cotton clothes to start. Don't assume anything in the beginning: your baby may be allergic to wool (many people are), and that beautiful sweater set Aunt Susie gave you at the baby shower may be very irritating to your little one.

Some clothing companies spray clothes with a product designed to keep the clothes from wrinkling while they are shipped to stores. So wash all baby clothes first, as well as bed sheets and baby blanket—anything that will be next to baby's skin. Down feathers are another potential hazard. Try allergy-friendly products first, then gradually, if you're not seeing skin rashes or other signs of allergic reactions, try other products, one at a time.

In addition to buying the usual clothes, diapers, and bedding, consider how some other products can help enhance attachment. Snuggly baby carriers (like the Mayawrap, found at www.mayawrap.com) keep the baby close to you during your day and can be invaluable in promoting attachment. Certain CDs and cassettes can enhance the emotion in which you hope you and your child will be engaging at different times of the day. For example, when it's cuddle time, you may want to play music such as *Songs for I Love You Rituals* by Mark Harmann. "By combining touch and music in an atmosphere of love, optimal brain development is supported" (Bailey 2000).

You will want to have soft, cuddly stuffed animals around, but not too many. Remember that *you* are the best cuddly-toy your child can have. However, as a transitional object, you may wish to find a cuddly stuffed animal or blanket your child seems to like, then tuck it under your arm for a few days as you go about your daily affairs, or sleep with it next to you. Gradually it will pick up your smell, and when you need to be away from your baby, or your little one needs to self-soothe, this transitional object can fill in.

ITEMS FROM YOUR BABY'S HOME

A wonderful way to ease the transition home is to have some familiar objects for your child. Here are some suggestions:

1. Ask those caring for your child before adoption to give you your daughter's old clothes, not the new, fancy clothes in which they dressed her up to meet her new family. Many times institutions dress the baby up so that she will look "American" or acceptable to her new family. As I mentioned before, you might send soft, comfortable clothes to your child ahead of time so she will have a chance to transition into her new wardrobe. However, if

this could not happen, ask the adoption agency to keep the baby in her normal clothes. You could even ask for a set or two of the clothes the baby is used to. The institution may demur, saying the old clothes are gone or dirty. Be persistent and even offer a few dollars if it would help. Then put these clothes back on your daughter even before you leave the institution or place where your daughter has been living. You may have to wait until they take "official pictures" of everyone smiling in new "dress-up" clothes before they allow you to change her. After you bring her home and she has had time to relax and get used to her new family and surroundings, you can begin to introduce new clothes that will have a different texture and smell.

2. Ask for her blanket, pillow, pacifier, bottle, sippy-cup, or anything else that was part of her eating, drinking, and sleeping routine. Again, they may give you a hard time or tell you they've thrown them away. Persist; again, offer a few dollars if you think that will work. You may even tell them you had some with you but they were lost on the plane—you're desperate and they're really helping you out! You need those things that are most familiar and "safe" to your baby.

3. This one may be fun and very complimentary to the caregivers who have been taking care of your daughter until you came to "claim" her. Bring an audio or videotape recorder, and ask to tape the caregiver holding the baby and singing, crooning, or even just talking to the baby in her native language. You will never regret having this tape. As soon as you get home, make a few copies and put at least one in the safe deposit box. In the meantime, make sure that the recording is available to you in the hotel and during the trip. A simple audiocassette tape recorder may be easiest to use unless you're proficient in managing video equipment and can easily carry it on the plane with you. Your baby's association with the orphanage or early placement may be traumatic. She may never want to hear the tapes again or may need intensive therapeutic help before she can hear the sounds without being thrown back into the terror of her life before she came to you. But you don't know that at the time you meet your little one and bring

her home. Many children, adopted or not, want to know at some point in their lives what their early months or years were like. If you don't collect and keep these historic pieces of information, you or your daughter will never have the choice of whether or not to revisit the experience. *Note:* What you're trying to secure here is the familiar sound that your child will recognize as the sound of safety. Don't take it personally that your child is not automatically comforted by the sound of your voice. Even if you adopt from the United States or another English-speaking country, accents are quite different, and many sounds just don't translate well. Your daughter needs to make this transition slowly to feel secure in her new environment.

4. Have you ever eaten at a foreign restaurant, where the foods are different and sometimes unpalatable? Or have you ever come home from eating foods that are new to you to find your intestinal track in an uproar? For many babies, American food (or food from your region of the country) is foreign and most likely represents a complete change in diet. The textures and tastes of our food are probably very different from what she knows. She may not like it, or it may make her ill. Therefore, until you know what your child likes and can easily tolerate, feed her as much of her native diet as you can. Try bringing food from the child's own country. Then introduce new foods carefully, going first with foods that are more or less safe. With the babies born to us, we introduce solid foods slowly so their little palates are mature enough to handle the different textures and tastes, and their gastrointestinal organs are ready to change from pure liquids to solids. So it should be with these little ones.

5. For many infants and toddlers in substandard care, feeding has been reduced to whatever is most convenient to the caregivers, not what is most appropriate to the children's development. For example, in an orphanage in Romania (and I understand this is also common in many institutions and foster care settings), children up to ages four and five are fed a thick oatmeal substance as their main food. In this particular institution the oatmeal is given to the children in their cribs in bottles with the top of the nipple

cut off, so the children can suck the oatmeal directly into their mouths—no messy utensils, no spilling food, no moving them from bed to table and back; easy delivery. The problem? There are many.

Proper gum and tooth development depends to a great extent on chewing. Oatmeal from a bottle? No chewing. Learning to use utensils to eat requires motor regulation, practice in hand-eye coordination, and such. No utensils? This creates a deficit in the practice of several important developmental skills. Sitting at a table, holding yourself upright, balancing as you master the art of feeding yourself—all important for motor, muscle, balance, and general physical development. Dental decay is rampant among children not properly fed. Watch your child for signs of low muscle tone, poor balance and underdeveloped hand-eye coordination, and especially poor dentition. You may need medical advice right away to learn how to help your child catch up or repair early problems.

However, a *strong* word of caution. If extensive dental (or other) medical repair work is indicated, do not let medical personnel anesthetize your child without you being present, at least in the pre- and postoperative settings. Best yet, have procedures done with the child in your lap or with you sitting or lying next to your child.

ABOUT SUSAN

At age seven days, Susan was found abandoned in a box at a detention center in China and was taken to an orphanage. She was premature, malnourished, and lethargic to the point of being catatonic. She was adopted at age five months by a non-Asian couple. Her father had two adult sons from a previous marriage. At age four and a half, she started attachment therapy. When asked "What do you wish you knew before adoption? What would you like preadoptive parents to know?" this is some of what this adoptive mom said.

> Here are things I wish someone had shared with us: Talk about separation and the effects no matter how perfect the foster care was. We were lulled into thinking that all the care was super in China and the babies will have no after-effects! All parents should understand how to help the child grieve, and how to bond no matter what the conditions of the adoptions.
>
> Make sure parents are prepared for the usual parenting stressors such as sleep deprivation, time changes, food allergies, people visiting, home issues, work issues, and how to prepare for the attachment phase and what it takes. Also list alternative preparations for working mothers, like "Stay home and take a sabbatical!"

6

Bringing Your
Baby Home

When we brought our new daughter home, we invited EVERYONE in the family to Kennedy Airport to meet her and help us celebrate. Cousins I hadn't seen since we were kids made the trek and played "pass the baby." It wasn't until hours later that I realized I hadn't held my own new baby since I couldn't remember when.

—Mother of two daughters adopted from Russia

I had always wanted a sister, someone to do things with. What I hadn't counted on was that I wouldn't like or even get along with my new sister. When I first met her, I didn't like her. At that point it was probably jealousy from being an only child for twelve years and then having to share my parents' love and affection. As time went along I didn't like her because we were and still are two very different people. After much trial and such, I can now say that I love her.

As for being the sibling, I could watch and observe everything that happened without being very emotionally involved. This has given me a unique perspective on our situation. In the beginning, when she was first visiting, she was pleasant and behaved for the most part. As time went along and she became more comfortable with the family, some of her aggression and past problems came out in the form of tantrums. I was not really prepared for these and they caught me off guard. But like all things, I got used to this after time. With therapy and as she got more attached to my mom, the tantrums became less and less frequent. In general, I believe she is more attached and capable as a human being of relating to others appropriately. Of course she still has a ways to go, but improvement has been made.

I can say honestly I believe that one day she will be perfectly normal. She will be different from me but that is just because we are different people with different personalities, and from different backrounds, not because she has emotional difficulties. It may have taken me three years to recognize the improvement and change in her, but when I look back I see baby steps that led to the leap of an improvement that I can now see.

—LETTER BY AN OLDER "BIRTH DAUGHTER" IN A
FAMILY WITH A YOUNGER SISTER ADOPTED AT AGE 9

The transition period from the adoption agency to your home, if handled correctly, can lay the groundwork for healthy attachment. It can be the first "proving ground" for your new son, helping him to understand that you are attuned to his needs and willing to put them before your own. On the other hand, your already skeptical child's first impression of you could be that you don't know how to take care of him—something he has most likely already experienced with the previous adults in his life.

For many new adoptive parents, homecoming is the time when they begin to wonder "what am I doing wrong?" when they could be thinking "this might be difficult for this beautiful little creature we now call 'ours' —how can I make this transition easier for him?"

Sound like a challenge? It should. But this chapter will give you ways to improve the odds dramatically so that this will be a healthy transition to a secure attachment.

Many well-meaning adoptive parents think their love alone is strong enough to overcome early problems. But if there are attachment issues you must remember they are a "hardwired" problem in the child's brain brought on by his or her early traumas. A medical analogy is apt here. Consider a growing child with a broken leg. If the leg is not treated correctly, it will most likely not heal properly, and this will eventually affect every part of the child's body. With proper treatment and follow-up, the leg will heal and the child will be whole again, although there will always be a scar. This is an analogy for attachment disorder.

To treat attachment disorder, you as parents must promote bonding with the adopted child in absolutely everything you do. You must work deliberately and creatively to nurture a feeling of safety and security in your child, and you must match your protective and nurturing actions to your loving words. For an older child, treatment can even include providing the vital stimulation that the child was not given as a baby—to the point of playing baby games like peekaboo or singing lullabies with even a six- or ten-year-old!

WHAT YOUR BABY IS FEELING WHEN YOU BRING HIM HOME

If yours is an international adoption, you will most likely be going to a county where you don't know much of the language (many parents learn at least a few words or phrases before going) and are not sure you can trust the food or medical care. How do you prepare? What clothing or emergency items do you take? What do you do when you can't be sure you can meet the needs of yourself, much less those of your new little one?

Your child is feeling apprehension about these same questions. If he is an infant and doesn't understand language, he is feeling the excitement or tension of being made ready for his new parents. If he is old enough to understand, he is being told that he is soon going to go to a new home with people he doesn't know.

He doesn't think like an adult, so he can't understand why he's feeling worried or anxious. He doesn't have your power to make himself safe: he can't pack an extra set of clothes, bring mix-with-water-and-stir soup in case the food is not palatable to him, or be sure the emergency medical kit has the right medicine if he feels "the runs" coming on.

In other words, he's stuck at the mercy of someone he doesn't know and has, basically, no reason to trust. Of course you're safe, smart, and resourceful and have made a commitment to do anything and everything in your power to protect and care for this child. But *he doesn't have any reason on earth to know this or to trust you.* Remember, this is a child whose trust has already been broken at least once, having been separated from his birth mother, and most likely again by being placed in the care of people who did not meet his needs.

He may well be terrified and scream himself blue in the face, not allowing himself to be comforted no matter what you do. If he seems inconsolable, do not play "pass the baby." This is an opportunity (one of many to come) for Mom to show the baby that she is ready, willing, and able to handle her baby's emotional pain without giving up. This is a key lesson for the baby to learn.

On the other hand, the baby may be resigned to the idea that, again, his needs are going to be ignored, so he might as well not even voice them. Rather than doing what babies usually do when they need something— cry, scream, or otherwise demand that they be cared for—he may lie quiet almost to the point of dormancy, having already given up hope.

Some parents tell me that they had no idea what was in store for them because their child was "so calm, he slept all the way home on the plane—all eighteen hours of the trip!" Depending on the child's age, this may be a reasonable thing for your son's little body to do. He has just been through the exhausting experience of being handed back and forth between adults, feeling the excitement yet high tension that you (and probably the government official or institution caregiver) have been feeling. These amazing little ones are highly tuned in to tension! For infants and young children, sleep can be a blessed relief from the panic they feel or the uncertainty they perceive around them.

In the face of this life-changing situation, don't have overly high expectations for your baby's response. You are now this child's parents. You must be there for the child, through rough times as well as happy moments. This trip from old home to new environment is stressful for your new child, even if it is in some ways "good stress" that your son is experiencing. Elizabeth Goff, M.D., of Allentown, Pennsylvania, is a pediatrician and a mother of two girls adopted from China. She notes, "Many adoptive parents picture the moment when they will first receive their baby as being a moment of great joy. Your baby will probably not feel that way. Her experience will range from neutral to traumatic. The joy will come later. Don't worry if your major feeling is anxiety and stress and if you don't feel connected to your baby at first. Attachment [most often] is not a sudden thing. It is a process, a relationship that happens over time."

Your job, however, is *attunement*—"tuning in" to what your child is feeling, how you can emotionally match that feeling, and doing what you need to do to meet your child's needs.

If you are adopting an older child, he may well be looking forward to being in his new family. However, he will still be worried that you may not like him or that he may not like you. He doesn't know whether he will please you or if you will keep him. Numerous times in my practice I have listened to tearful children admit that they have been afraid *since the beginning* that they would be again abandoned, passed on to another family, or just plain "given away." This is true of many adopted children, no matter how many times Forever Parents tell their child they will not give him away. And if you ask your child if it is true for him—if he is afraid you will give him away, he will probably say no, at least in the early years of being yours. Children do not always understand the source of their anxiety or fears. But trust me, these fears are there and very real.

HOW TO HANDLE THE HOMECOMING

I wish they had given us a handbook or pamphlet of do's and don'ts regarding caring for our son immediately after we got him.

—MOTHER OF A BOY ADOPTED FROM RUSSIA AT AGE FIVE

The story at the beginning of the chapter—of the family reunion at Kennedy International—is an example of what *not* to do when you bring your baby home. It seems counterintuitive, because to us, celebrating such a happy event involves lots of people and laughter and hubbub. And doesn't everyone in the extended family want to show their love for the new baby by holding her, cuddling her, cooing at her, and trying to engage her in a collective celebration?

But look at it from the baby's point of view. A common misconception is that the baby will be "excited" about coming to her new home. In fact, the baby will probably be frightened by the new *sensory bath* in which she finds herself. All of a sudden, after a lengthy journey, she is being thrust into a crowd of many new and unfamiliar smells, sounds, and strange bodies. I can only guess that it must be like running a gauntlet in which she doesn't know which member of the "torture team" is going to be the one with the poison sword. Remember what we said earlier about babies' stress levels when they are removed from their mothers or placed in unfamiliar arms or places?

The baby should have as much serenity as possible and *must* be in Mom's (or Dad's) arms the entire time. Seriously: the baby should not be out of Mom's arms for several days, twenty-four hours a day, except maybe for sleep and bathroom breaks. This 24/7 closeness can form the basis for healthy attaching. Even if your new daughter is crying pretty much nonstop, Cousin Pat should not take the baby from Mom in an effort to help. This is a very early chance for the Forever Parents to exhibit what I call "unconditional being with": showing the baby that they will stick with her through even this frightening and exhausting experience.

Make everything as simple and peaceful as possible for you and the new baby. That may mean having your parents meet you at the airport to help you with luggage and drive you home so you don't have to find the car in the gigantic parking lot and spend lots of time in sleet and snow or extremely hot temperatures. The hordes of family and friends eager to meet the new family member will have plenty of time to welcome the baby when the time is right. Now is the time for the baby to be learning to accept the new sensory input that is bombarding her from all sides without having to worry about pleasing people she doesn't know.

Dr. Goff advises, "You will be exhausted and stressed from travel, and all of your sleep schedules will be off. Resist the attempts of well-meaning friends and relatives to plan a welcome-home party or for all to arrive to greet you at the airport. Keep this transition as quiet and as low stress as possible. If your baby was in an orphanage, she may be perfectly happy to be passed around the room at a party, but this is not a good idea for her attachment formation. Limit your baby's interaction to only the most important close family members at first, and ask everyone else to be patient." By the way, these admonitions are equally true if you are adopting domestically, and may be bringing your child home from only a few blocks away. Keep homecoming simple, low-key, stress-free, and as relaxed as possible.

If need be, a close friend or understanding family member can help with "reentry" into the country and making your way home, but make sure she or he is aware of the importance of bonding between mother and baby first. Relatives and friends who are unaware of the importance of attachment can do more harm than good with their well-meaning attempts to relieve Mom of her baby duties. Let them know that they can support you best by leaving you alone—or at best, taking care of you and your family—while you do this important work. You may have to be firm about it!

Just as with helping any family with a new baby, friends and family can be supportive in many ways. Ask them to fix a meal for you. Perhaps a friend can help with cleaning, shopping, or laundry. A close friend or family member might make arrangements to take older siblings for short but special outings or to help with homework or games at home. Accept offers of help.

While there is no hard and fast rule that I know of, some professionals believe you can expect that it will take about one week of intense attaching to "make up" for each month that your child was alive before she came to be with you. I am careful to avoid making predictions, because each child is so very individual. But you may see a similar type of time formula in some books on attachment, and we may find, in the end, that there is some truth to it. Just don't let the numbers discourage you if your situation doesn't fit neatly into someone else's predictions.

Be prepared, also, for the experience some call the "honeymoon period." For many children with attachment problems they have learned to be "people pleasers" in order to have their needs met. They smile and coo at new adults, almost flirting—in effect trying to win over the affection of the adult.

However, much like being an actor on a stage, putting on this show is exhausting and stressful in itself and cannot last forever (though in a few extraordinary cases I have seen this last up to six months!). Eventually, the child's ability to sustain this show gives out. Then the negative behaviors associated with attachment problems begin to surface, sometimes with a vengeance.

What about siblings? Reread the letter at the beginning of this chapter written by a particularly precocious older birth sibling in an adoptive family. Siblings should be waiting at home and should be helped to understand that they can be happy to meet and greet the new baby, but the baby needs to stay with Mom.

Siblings might be happy to support the mother-baby attachment experience, or they may feel left out, jealous, or frightened that they may be losing their place in the family. Pay attention to your other children as much as you can. This may be another instance in which good friends or extended family can play an important role, too. Perhaps they can plan an outing or special activities with the other children in the family.

On the other hand, I would think very cautiously about sending them away—to a relative's home out of town or sleepover camp—during this transition period unless that is what usually happens at that particular time of year. I'm not saying categorically that you shouldn't do it. I'm simply advising you to be very careful lest your other children feel angry and anxious from being so far away from you.

ONCE YOUR CHILD IS HOME

What can you do to promote attachment with your new child once she is settled in her new home? Please consider the following recommendations carefully, even if you don't believe your child has any attachment issues or if you are adopting from a culture similar to our own and feel there should be no problem. What can you lose by being respectful of the dramatic changes you are asking your daughter to accept?

Think about it. You as parents are introducing only one new change into your lives and family (albeit a very important change!). But your new daughter is experiencing a massive and abrupt change in her little life and sense of security, with suddenly all new expectations in life, including becoming accustomed to new sights, smells, sounds, tastes, temperatures, routines, and tactile sensations; meeting and learning to know an entirely new family; and grieving the loss of her old life.

During the first few days you will begin to understand your new child, just as birth parents do. Right now the baby should be surrounded by two things: one is as many feelings and smells as were natural in her native home, and the second is Mom. These are the only things that we want the baby to be interpreting through her senses. The transition is shocking enough as it is, given that we cannot screen out things like sounds and the ways the air smells. Keep everything as familiar as possible; the only major change you should be introducing at this point is Mom. This is the best way to begin the transition to a new attachment. In a very real sense, you are letting your baby begin to make up for the nine months of living in Mom's womb that she will never have with you; it's a time of security and bonding.

Dr. Goff suggests that one parent take on the role of "first attacher" during this intial period:

> Many experts on attachment and adoption recommend that you choose which parent will be the "first attacher." This is because babies do their best attaching to one person at a time. Once your baby attaches well to the first parent, then she will attach to the second parent. The first attacher, as much as possible, should give the bottles, change the diapers, do the comforting, and do a lot of carrying and holding. The other parent initially should take the role of assistant, supporter, and pack mule. Don't worry, your baby will grow to love you too; just be a little patient. Remember, this is just an ideal. Realistically, the first attacher may get sick, develop a back spasm, etc. Then you have to improvise, keeping the needs of the baby as your primary concern. (Goff 2002)

There is no timetable for allowing a child to begin to attach with someone other than the first attacher. In fact, the nature or experiences of a few children may allow for the child to form more than one at a time, but don't count on that happening. But just as there is no exact timetable for when an infant gradually can handle solid foods in his or her diet or successfully complete potty training, there is no exact timetable for when the baby can begin to experience fulfillment, rather than stress, in completing the process of attaching to more than one trusted adult.

Use your instincts, even to the point of trying things like leaving the baby with the second attacher for very short periods to see the reaction and then backing off if it's clearly too much. And if you are left with concerns, seek professional help.

Remember that babies or young children can't tell you how they're really feeling. Making "sleuthing" even more difficult is the fact that "symptoms in children also look different than they do in adults. While a depressed thirty-five-year-old may say, 'I feel worthless,' or 'I have no energy,' a child might say he feels bored and isn't having much fun" (Hochman 2003).

PRACTICAL TRANSITION TIPS ONCE YOUR CHILD IS HOME

Give your new baby as much help as you can by trying to minimize changes and making a slow, gradual transition. Here are some other, practical suggestions to ease the transition:

- Wear soft clothing that will feel good to your baby.
- Keep your brand of shampoo, deodorant, and so on consistent to minimize changes in how you smell to your baby.
- Wear a baby carrier (like the Mayawrap) to keep your baby close to you as much as possible.
- Talk softly and often to your baby, play gently and carefully with your baby, and encourage eye contact.
- Respond to your baby's needs promptly. Don't worry about "developing bad habits" or "spoiling." The first priority is attachment. Remember, this is a dance: she leads, you respond.
- Make an appointment with a pediatrician as soon as possible. Your baby should be screened for a number of illnesses, such as skin problems, intestinal problems, tuberculosis, and infections. Here is

another chance for Mom to show the baby that Mom can and will take care of whatever is giving the baby pain. See chapter 8 for details on the medical problems that these children may bring with them.

- Having your baby sleep with you is a great way to start the attachment process. This is a situation in which conventional wisdom about having the child sleep in a crib is just not appropriate. Second best is having the baby in a crib or on a mat next to your bed. If you "co-sleep," keep the blankets low by your waist, away from the baby's face. Dress your baby warmly enough to not need blankets, and keep pillows away from his face.

HOW YOUR BABY RESPONDS TO YOU

Your baby's initial response to you is influenced largely by the way in which she has been cared for up to this point in her life. If her cries were not consistently responded to at the orphanage, "the baby may not cry much and may not give you very clear cues about what she needs. She may not be comfortable with eye contact and may prefer to be held facing outward. She may feel awkward to carry, tending to be more rigid rather than molding herself to you," according to Dr. Goff.

If her cries were responded to, but by multiple caregivers, "this baby is likely to be happy and outgoing. She may initially seem pretty well adjusted because she will probably be comfortable with you and will accept care readily. From her point of view, you may be just another of a large number of caregivers. It may be a while before she starts to understand that you are 'it,'" says Dr. Goff.

The response of the child who was in foster care varies based on age and developmental level, Dr. Goff explains:

A baby under 6–7 months may be somewhat sad and withdrawn but is likely to recover relatively quickly and attach well. If your child is in the age range when separation anxiety normally develops (8–12 months), she may seem panicked. Children in this stage who are well-attached cry with great anxiety when their mother goes out of sight. Imagine what it is like to be in this stage and then have your mother (remember, the baby didn't know that the foster mother was temporary) suddenly disappear and never come back. This baby is experiencing shock and bereavement. She may cry inconsolably, have disrupted sleep, feed poorly for a while and become constipated. (Body chemicals released during stress such as epinephrine can cause constipation.) . . . it is likely that the time it takes to see early signs of attachment will be shortest for the baby in good foster care and longest for the baby whose cries were not responded to.

Here's a very lovely connection you and your little one can have that may have a wonderfully calming and "attaching" effect. Remember when you were little and you were tired but something inside of you needed "calming" before you could slip into a restful night's sleep? And remember when Mom or Dad (or a favorite grandparent or older sibling or whoever) would sit by the side of your bed, give you a big, warm hug, and tell you everything would be all right? There's not much in the world like it, frankly, even for adults.

So imagine your new little one is upset, frightened, lonely, or just unsure about things and doesn't know how to express the upset feelings—she is too young, or doesn't know the language, or is too locked up inside or *basically dysregulated* to say or even know what she's feeling. Now imagine that you and your child are in some special place where you won't be interrupted, and you can rock her, sing to her, or even better, just hold her to your chest for one very important reason: she should come to the state of relaxation where she can hear your heartbeat. This state of calm "connection" will bring her back to a prebirth time when she was safely enfolded in her mother's womb, where she was aware only of being totally cared for. In this relaxed, attuned place, with your little one hearing your heartbeat much as we listen to the surf pounding on the shore, she may feel safe again, secure in *you*, and now associating *you* with that place of security.

If you can attain this beautiful state of attunement, simply relax into it yourself. Now you can begin a new level of attachment—being with each other in a profoundly connected way. Don't be afraid or upset if this time of relaxed attunement doesn't come until after what feels like a long, hard cry. Sometimes dysregulated babies and children need to "cry it out" before they can relax and be comforted. Just stay calm and reassure yourself—that's really the key.

PRESERVING YOUR CHILD'S HERITAGE

Gather as much culture as you can in the country of origin. Learn the language if possible, even a few phrases. And bring home as many little gifts as you can for the child as she grows.

—MOTHER OF TWO GIRLS ADOPTED FROM CHINA

EMILY'S STORY

The father of one of our families wrote this beautiful story for his adopted daughter and has given us permission to share it.

Once upon a time, on the side of a mountain in China, a Beautiful Baby Girl was born. It was on a bright, sunny day in February, and the baby had big brown eyes, dark silky hair, a cute smile, and soft, smooth skin.

When the Beautiful Baby Girl was born, her parents were very happy, but also worried. For the China Mom and Dad were very poor. They were farmers who did not have enough money to take care of her.

So they talked for days and days and made a very hard decision. They decided it would be better if their Beautiful Baby Girl lived with another family, a family that could care for her, and parents who would give her everything she needed in life and, of course, love her.

Late that night, after dinner, Mom and Dad fed the Beautiful Baby Girl and carried her outside for a walk. The three of them stood on the top of a mountain near their village and sat on an old dead tree to enjoy the lovely sunset with their Baby. The Mom and Dad hugged each other and their Baby. They had tears of joy and sadness because they knew they were doing the right thing, but they also knew they would miss the Beautiful Baby Girl very much.

The Mommy looked at the Beautiful Baby Girl and said, "You will never be away from my thoughts, Little One. Every time you stop to enjoy a sunset with your Forever Mom, wherever you are in the world, I'll be looking at the same sun from the top of our mountain and thanking God you are happy and well."

They wrapped the Beautiful Baby Girl in some warm clothes and a soft, freshly cleaned blanket that the Mom had knitted for her, and put her in a strong wooden open box that the Dad had made, with a can of milk and a note. The note said, "This is our daughter and we love her very much; please take care of her and love her as we do."

The three of them went over to the other side of the mountain. Birth Mom and Dad put the box with the Beautiful Baby Girl where they knew someone would quickly find her. Then they ran around the corner and peeked, waiting to make sure someone would find her.

Soon a strong, kind policeman was walking by and saw the wooden box with the Beautiful Baby Girl inside. He picked her up, read the note and looked around to see if he could find anyone who knew where this special treasure had come from. Then he sat down on the steps and fed the Beautiful Baby Girl her bottle of milk.

The Beautiful Baby Girl burped and looked up, smiling at the kind policeman's friendly face. She liked his bright eyes and the shiny badge on his hat.

The kind policeman read the note again and kissed the little Baby on her forehead. He said, "Your Mommy and Daddy must love you very much."

Around the corner, the parents were happy to see that someone had found their Baby and was already taking care of her. They walked away and had tears of joy and sadness. They were sad to see their daughter leave them but were happy knowing she would have a wonderful life.

The kind policeman carried the Beautiful Baby Girl around the corner to a special home for little children.

The Baby was not used to being around so many other babies and so much noise! She was so tiny she could not talk yet in words, so no one understood that she was frightened. No one could tell when she wanted to be picked up or held or have songs sung to her. She had a rattle that she held onto all the time, except when she put the rattle down so she could cover her ears to block out the noise.

Because there were so many other babies with her, the little Baby did not get picked up and held as much as she wanted or needed. She did not think anyone loved her, or that she was important enough to be loved. She was sad, but no one at the special home for children knew how sad she had become.

The Beautiful Baby Girl lay in her crib. She stayed about five long months with the other children. She was just like Madeline, who was living with her eleven friends in a home in Paris, in a house all covered with vines. Except this baby wasn't happy; not happy at all.

One day in the spring, when there was another lovely sunset, an important official in China came running in with some exciting news. He had received a letter from a Mom and Dad in America. They had heard about the Beautiful Baby Girl who was living in the special home for children in China. They wanted very much for her to come to live with them. They asked the important official in China if they could fly over to China and bring her back with them, as soon as possible. The important official said yes!

Now, as it happens, at that instant the Beautiful Baby Girl's China Mom, who knew she could not take care of the little Baby after she was born, was standing on top of her special hill. She was watching the lovely sunset and was praying to God, hoping that her little Baby was being cared for and loved.

Just then, God whispered to her that her prayers were answered and that her daughter would soon be going off to America to live with her Forever Mommy and Daddy, who would love her, take care of her, keep her safe, and give her everything she needed in life.

The China Mother fell to her knees and cried tears of joy and relief. She looked up at the sunset and thanked God.

Everyone back at the special home for children was happy for the Beautiful Baby Girl. They were going to be sad to see her leave, but they knew she would be better off living with a real family who could take care of her.

Since the Beautiful Baby Girl could not talk yet, no one knew what she was thinking. But what she thought to herself was, "I'm going to be safe now. I'm going to have my own family who can take care of me besides loving me. I'm going to have the family my Birth Mom and Dad wanted me to have. It will be scary at first because I don't know them, but then it will be fine. I will be safe and fine and OK and loved. And I will belong to them!"

A few weeks later, Forever Mommy and Daddy arrived in China. The woman who was taking care of the Beautiful Baby Girl brought her to them at the hotel where they were staying, close to the special home for children.

Carefully, gently, the Beautiful Baby Girl was put into her Forever Mommy's arms. Forever Mom cradled her new Little One in her arms and tears of joy ran down her face. She had been waiting her whole life for this Beautiful Baby Girl to be her very own baby!

Forever Mommy gave her Beautiful Baby Girl a bath, put fresh clothes on her, and gave the thirsty baby some milk. Baby was so thirsty she quickly drank two bottles of milk and then let own a really loud burp! She looked up proudly and smiled at her Forever Mom.

The next day was warm and sunny and the new, happy family went for a walk. Later that day, Forever Mommy went for another walk alone with her new daughter. She was hoping to see a sunset.

At the far end of town, Forever Mommy sat down on a park bench and looked into her Beautiful Baby Girl's bright, warm brown eyes and told her how very much she loved her and that she was going to take care of her forever. She sang her a song. She told her daughter that she knew how to take care of her new Little One. She said a prayer of thanks to God and looked up to see the loveliest sunset she'd ever seen. A ray of sunlight came through the trees and landed on the Baby's little head.

Miles away, on the other side of the mountain, the Baby's China Mother was looking at the same sunset. Somehow, in some way, she knew her little Baby Girl was safe, and now she could finally be happy. She smiled the wonderful smile that Moms smile when their babies are safe and happy.

The new Forever Family flew back to America three days later, back to their home, safe and sound. And now Forever After, they belong together; her Forever Mommy and Daddy love her most of all, and she loves them.

7

PARENTING TO ENHANCE ATTACHMENT

I wish I had followed my own instincts [to keep baby close in a sling, in bed, etc.] instead of taking the advice of well-meaning relatives and others who had lots of parenting experience but who had no adopted children. And I wish I had continued to search for the right therapist even after the daunting, countless experiences of yet another therapist who had no clue of what my baby and I were going through and so blamed me.

—MOTHER OF JADE, A GIRL ADOPTED FROM KOREA

Now you're ready to begin the actual experience of living with your new child. You may be exhausted, somewhat frustrated, and possibly a bit discouraged that your long-awaited blessed event isn't exactly like the movies, or like your neighbors, who smiled nonstop from the time their new child came home with them. You're also still in awe that this child, this beautiful bundle of nerves, energy, and joy, has come to be yours. But you're beginning to notice little things that make you wonder, and maybe worry.

This chapter is a practical one, highlighting common problems and frequently voiced concerns about attachment and other problems in the adoptive-parenting process. We will discuss the critical importance of planning and conscientiously continuing to perform attachment activities with your child.

FOSTERING ATTACHMENT: THE BASICS

I wish we had been required to take some classes on attachment after we adopted our son. We could have helped him so much more if we had realized how much he needed us to control his life; how much structure, routine, rituals, and nurturing activities he needed to feel really safe and secure.

—MOTHER OF A BOY ADOPTED FROM RUSSIA

Our primary job as parents is *not* to be our child's "buddy" or "best friend," at least not in the traditional sense of those terms. Throughout their lives they will have various buddies and best friends; they will, if they are lucky, always have us as their parents. Whether we are birth, step, foster, or "Forever" parents, we play a unique role in their lives. We should not confuse our job; if we do, our children will lose out on receiving the most precious gift we can offer them—ourselves as people who happily and lovingly sacrifice a great portion of our lives to give them the structure and nurture that is every child's birthright.

What this means in practical terms is that we have a job to do that includes setting very clear and enforceable boundaries for our children's growing-up years. It means we have to make ourselves available and consistent in enforcing those boundaries. It means we have to make tremendous sacrifices and give our children what *they* need, not what we feel like doing at the time. Parenting is often not fun (regardless of all the joy and satisfaction it brings), and it is absolutely demanding in every sense of the word.

Here's a simple, if not easy, fact: *You must try to make every action solidify the attachment between you and your child.* That holds true even if the activity seems embarrassing, silly, or restricting. In the early days with your child, you must make sure that you and she are not separated, she is not frightened, and you are seen as the ultimate protector of her safety and security. The goal is for your child to develop trust in you as the giver of all gifts and the person on whom all life is dependent (as was her birth mother in the beginning). You must become the lifeline for your child, the one she lost when the bond was broken between her and her birth parents.

Your child needs to be nurtured. She needs to feel and experience what it is like to be totally relaxed with and dependent on a person who is trustworthy enough to allow this to happen safely. (Why do you think "babe" or "baby" are such common terms of endearment between family members, true friends, and lovers? Because they reflect this trusting, relaxed, state of emotional intimacy between two people.) This is the basis for attachment, and you need to incorporate this understanding into all of your thinking, feeling, and acting with your child.

For your child's neurological system to begin to heal and work properly again, she must first experience the feeling of total trust. Look around you the next time you are in an airport, at church, or someplace where there are lots of mothers, fathers, and infants. Watch the little ones who are asleep on Mommy or Daddy's shoulder. They are so totally relaxed and trusting, which is what makes it possible for them to give themselves over to this deep and restorative sleep. All of the activities in this chapter are designed to promote this trust.

CHILDREN THINK DIFFERENTLY

Even if you have raised children in the past and understand the effort involved, you must understand that adoption involves an entirely new set of rules. Some things are the same. We love our children, no matter what. We must accept them as the unique and wondrous little people they are. And we also have to understand that children—all children— think differently from the way adults do.

Psychologist John Tardibuono is a friend and colleague who has the gift of still thinking like a child when he works with them. We were recently discussing children's fears about the terrorist attacks on

September 11, 2001. We were talking about how children think of geography. John reminded me that no matter how well a child can memorize where the states go on a U.S. puzzle map, and regardless of how easily he can remember a route he may have traveled once from here to there, he has not yet developed an internal understanding of the concept of distance. Hearing about terrorists hiding "in the mountains of Afghanistan" may bring to mind a picture of "the mountains," three hours from home, where the family went camping on their vacation last summer. To your child, the terrorists may be as real as the people you all met while camping, and they most likely feel very close! It's difficult to persuade your child that Afghanistan is on the other side of the world and that terrorists will not be crawling into his bedroom window that very night after taking a short drive down the turnpike from "the mountains."

Let's say your otherwise healthy nine-year-old comes crying into your bedroom in the middle of the night, asking to crawl into bed with you. What do you do? You find out why the child is waking in distress, and then you help to "fix" the problem. In this situation, you might logically ask, "What are you afraid of?" and "Did you have a bad dream?"

But there is every chance that your son may not know what frightened him. Bad dreams have a way of disappearing when we come out of sleep and back into conscious thought. Children lack the adult framework that helps them distinguish between what is acceptable and what is frightening. Without that framework how do they know what is coming up in their bad dreams? Are they stored memories from long ago, or are they fears about current experiences or happenings? Even most of us as adults have trouble making sense of bad dreams. How can we expect youngsters to do so?

Especially when for children at risk for attachment problems, what is stored in their brains may be years of abuse and neglect and fear. To understand in depth how infant brains store memory and how the experiences and memories they provide impact a neurological development, read *The Developing Mind* by Daniel Siegel (1999). I refer to this book often because of the excellent job Dr. Siegel has done in making this information understandable.

Here's a concrete example. During the 1991 U.S. military operation known as "Desert Storm," I was principal of an elementary school.

Several mornings a week the teachers would bring their classes into the library, and we would talk about what the children might be seeing on television, reading in the newspapers, or hearing from their parents, friends, or neighbors about the war. We encouraged the children to ask questions in order to check the reality of what they *thought* they understood about the situation. No child's question was ridiculed, and no one's fears were taken lightly. Many of them began to be in touch with thoughts that might previously have been too upsetting for them to consciously consider, much less say out loud. They started to ask questions and actively seek answers about feelings or thoughts that had been buried or unexplored.

One morning a bright second-grader, who had been to many of these gatherings but had said nothing to this point, reluctantly raised her hand. I can still see the tears in her eyes and hear the quiver in her voice as she expressed her terror: "But Mrs. Eshleman, my best friend lives in Lebanon." Our school was in Lancaster, Pennsylvania, about twenty miles from a town called Lebanon (you may know it from its exceptionally good Lebanon bologna). This sweet, worried child had been hearing on the news about bombs and killing and war, and at some point the country of Lebanon was mentioned. All she knew was that her best friend lived in a place called Lebanon. At age seven, she was not equipped to tell the difference, or even ask the question, without some help. She felt but didn't completely understand the distress her parents were experiencing about the war. She didn't normally see her friend every week, so it hadn't been unusual that she hadn't seen her for the past few weeks. For all she knew, her friend had been bombed to death or was in terrible distress, without this child even knowing about it or being able to do anything to help.

How long had this poor child carried around the fear about her friend? How long did she struggle with the question before she felt safe enough to ask the question and find out what she feared might be the terrible answer? Did she have bad dreams or nightmares that she hadn't been able to even remember by morning, much less discuss rationally with parents? Might we have seen this little girl's distress if we had been more vigilant? Had her parents seen changes in her behavior at home and other settings outside of school? I called her parents to explain to them what happened in school that morning, as I have always believed that immediate and open communication between home and school is critical. The girl's parents had noticed that their daughter had been a little more quiet than usual but had attributed this to the general atmosphere of tension about the war.

This scenario is played out every day in healthy, well-functioning families with children who are in good shape for their age and level of development—and whose fears the parents can understand and usually know about. With many children adopted both domestically and from abroad there may be a higher risk for developmental delays and early emotional trauma—ones of which the parents may not even be aware. For these children, situational stressors—stressors in their environment—might be "more real" or feel more powerful than for most children. Furthermore, their ability to perform "reality checking" may well be impaired.

It is our job as parents to create a safe environment in which children can ask the questions about things that frighten or confuse them. We have to respect that children *do* think differently from adults and *do not* have the context in which to put certain thoughts or feelings in order to test them out.

But what about the children who are not ready or able to express their fears or even to identify them? For these children, what *we* think of as "no problem"—a car backfiring, a sideways glance by a man on a bus, breaking a dish by accident—carries with it a huge emotional component that shouts, "Danger! Be terrified!" As we've discussed in earlier chapters, for these children, needing to always be on extra alert has meant nothing short of survival.

How do we help these children learn what their feelings are? How do we give them a format in which to express those fears and have them relieved? This chapter gives suggestions on how to parent on a day-to-day basis to help your child overcome past traumas and current fears—and learn to trust and attach to you. We also begin to talk about the partnership between professional knowledge and guidance and therapeutic attachment parenting.

YOU WANT ME TO DO *WHAT?*

Many parents tell me early in therapy that many of the techniques I recommend seem wrong, uncomfortable, or even counterintuitive to them. That's understandable, because parenting a child at risk for attachment disorder in many ways is not the same as parenting a healthy child. The requirements for being the best possible parent for this child are often different, and so are the ways that we achieve being this "best parent." What worked with other children might not be the way to proceed with a child at risk for attachment disorder.

Elizabeth Goff, M.D., along with her partner, has adopted two girls from China. As she puts it, "The so-called common wisdom is often specifically wrong for these children. . . . The standard advice in terms of sleeping, feeding, discipline and catching up all is opposite." Here are some common recommendations for parenting a birth child without problems, and the reasons why they're not right for children with attachment problems:

1. "Have your child sleep alone." As we noted in chapter 6, it's best to have newly adopted children sleep with their parents. Physical presence is key (more about that below). Be prepared for sleep problems and nightmares. The child may not sleep through the night.

2. "Let your child cry." These children should be comforted immediately in an attempt to provide security and trust. If your child cries when put to bed at night, initially give her whatever she seems to need to quiet down and go to sleep. Don't be overly concerned about creating bad habits. Then transition her slowly from, for example, (1) needing to be rocked to sleep, to (2) being placed in the crib or bed awake but having you stay and pat her back, to (3) being placed in bed and having you sit across the room, to (4) having you leave the room and provide only verbal comfort, to (5) having the child put herself to sleep after a soothing bedtime ritual. Transition slowly. Wait until your child is well adjusted to one stage, then move to the next step. In time you will learn to discern your baby's different cries. You will know the dif-

ference between the "I'm annoyed that you're not giving me exactly what I want right now" cry (which should not be answered) and the "I'm really scared or distressed" cry (to which you should always respond with comfort)

3. "Monitor your child's developmental milestones." With these children, you don't want to push them ahead; instead, you actually want to regress in an attempt to heal the bond that was broken in infancy.

Dr. Daniel Hughes and most attachment therapists refer to these activities as part of a *planned regression*—a process of taking a child back to early developmental stages that she might have missed. We don't wait for the child to regress to an early state of dysregulation and dependency out of fear or shame. Instead, we as parents guide them back to that state and nurture them there, at that stage in life when they were *not* cared for properly, or *not* given the structure and nurture all infants and young children need.

Even if your child has been with you for quite a while, and came to you at a relatively young age, he or she might not have been able to accept the love you offered early on. It may have been like the story of the two children, each given positive reinforcement in the form of little handwritten notes which the children put in their pockets. The expectations would be, of course, that as the child receives lots of positive reinforcement and his pocket fills up, he develops a strong and positive self-concept.

But what if he has a hole in his pocket? What if his self-esteem is already so damaged or shaky that he doesn't even have a framework in which to fit or keep these positive reinforcers? Incorporating loving techniques into your parenting can help your child "sew up" that hole in his pocket and reorganize his self-concept to a more positive, lovable one.

Your child, when she was removed from her birth mother, experienced a break in normal bonding. Just as when we are rejected by a person very close to us emotionally, the experience can leave us extremely cautious of allowing ourselves to be vulnerable again. So, by virtue of the fact that you are now trying to form an attachment with her, she will try to push you away. Be ready for it. If you are not ready or do not have enough support, you will be confused and hurt by that rejection. You will back off, which seems the right thing to do. However, in forming attachments, backing off is exactly the wrong thing to do.

Some of these children may need to be taught such rudimentary skills as how to chew (they may have been given only bottles) or how to use the bathroom. Even up to the middle years in many preadoption institutions, children are kept in diapers to make things easier for staff. Often, too, when children are stressed, they regress by themselves. What seemed like well-learned behaviors just disappear, much to their parents' distress. We hear of this phenomenon often with toilet-trained toddlers when a new baby joins the family. And here Mom thought she would have only *one* baby's diapers to change!

In these situations, the parents need to learn how to feed the child, how to give medicine, how to potty train—or re-train—and how to provide nurturing physical touch through it all.

PROJECTING CONSISTENCY AND CONFIDENCE

Sometimes parents have trouble understanding why "regular" parenting isn't enough to overcome their child's built-up resistance to what would seem like "normal" and otherwise appropriate parenting. But imagine being a soldier in a war. You are especially nervous as you prepare for battle because in the last battle you had inept leaders. You were put in extreme danger because your leader was unable to direct you in ways to maximize your safety in war, which is, by definition, an unsafe situation. Your natural inclination is to expect that this is a dangerous battle for which you are preparing. You need strong, predictable, "prove-it-to-me" leadership before you commit yourself to yet another battle charge.

Now, imagine two different colonels giving you a prebattle pep talk. Here's the first: "Well, people, we are going to try our best to, um, you know, do this thing. We can probably do this, right? Is that okay with you? What do you think? Are you ready? We're just fine; at least I think we are. Yup, I'll bet we can be okay with this, don't you think?"

Here's the second colonel: "So, people, here's the plan. It will work, I know. This is your part, and I know you will do your best. I will lead you in, and I will stay with you—I will not desert you. We will win. You will be safe. Now let's GO!"

Amazing difference, isn't it? Take the second colonel as your role model for parenting. You don't have to be a drill sergeant, but you do have to be positive and assured, show your little one that you know what you're doing (even if, in fact, you're not feeling so terribly self-assured), and then go with it! Making a "mistake" (doing something you afterwards wished you had done differently), and then having to apologize and do it over in another fashion, is infinitely better than being wishy-washy with these little ones. They need assurance that you know what you're doing. As long as you're safe in whatever you're doing—as in keeping your child physically safe—you can model for your child that it is okay to make a mistake, apologize, regroup, and go on.

MAINTAINING PHYSICAL PRESENCE

In normal attachment, parents take certain steps to ensure that their children are safe and are developing according to nature's best plan. According to Daniel Hughes (1998), a noted attachment therapist and author from Maine, these steps have at their core the physical presence of the parent:

> Maintaining physical presence is the primary way that parents discipline toddlers. Parents are aware of their toddler. They "keep an eye on her" and "an ear on him" constantly throughout the day. They are near their child, so that the child takes their presence for granted and gradually comes to rely on their knowledge about what to do. Their child also constantly engages in "social referencing" whereby (s)he watches his/her parents' nonverbal reactions to know whether or not someone or something is a danger or is safe. The parents' presence gives the child the sense of safety necessary to be able to explore and learn about his/her world.

Hughes notes that children with attachment problems "need physical presence just as much as does the toddler. They do not have the skills needed to internalize rules, control impulses, remember consequences of their actions, have empathy for others, or feel safe. Allowing them to be outside of their parents' presence, to make the 'right' choice unsupervised, is a blueprint for disaster and failure."

According to Hughes, physical presence involves two main components: (1) structure and containment and (2) fun and love. Structure and containment refer to these elements:

1. Supervision: The parent is aware of the child at all times when he is not sleeping. If the parent is out of visual contact briefly, the child is confined to an area (with a door alarm if necessary) where he cannot hurt himself or destroy something important.
2. Nearness: The child sits, plays, works, or rests near his parent. The parent enjoys his company, frequently with brief engagements.
3. Routine: There is a well-defined routine, alternating active and quiet activities, work and play, solitary and interactive activities.
4. Limited choice: The parent chooses the activities as well as much of the food, clothing, toys, and so on for the child, giving him the ability to choose only when he shows some readiness to make good choices.
5. Safety: The home is childproof, even for older children.

The fun and love aspects of physical presence arise when the parent provides numerous activities to become engaged in with her child with reciprocal fun and affection. The parent is attuned to the child's emotional state and is engaged with her in positive emotional, nonverbal communication throughout. These activities might include the following for attachment-impaired children:

1. Feed the child and give him a bottle, as you would an infant or toddler
2. Hold, rock, hug, touch, massage him
3. Roll, crawl, and rest among pillows on the floor with him
4. Sing songs and play games
5. Play habitual background music
6. Wash him, dress him, and comb his hair
7. Read and tell stories
8. Enjoy quiet, extended bedtime routines
9. Go for a walk, holding hands
10. Have periods of "baby talk" and "small talk"

INTERPRETING MISBEHAVIOR
AND "READING" YOUR CHILD

Let's look at the word "misbehave" for a moment. What it means is that this child is behaving in a way we believe is incorrect or unacceptable. But isn't that awfully subjective? Every family has its own opinions about what constitutes "misbehavior." I have seen parents who are perfectly comfortable with their child hitting other people, scratching themselves in "private parts" in public, or telling adults to "shut up" or "go away." Other parents expect their children to be quiet and submissive to adults, to follow every directive immediately and without question, and to never hit or say "shut up" to anyone, much less an adult.

So what do we use as a measure of misbehavior? I suggest we look behind the behavior to what it represents: what is the child really trying to tell us?

Imagine for a minute that you have a new, cute little puppy, say a soft furball of a yellow labrador called Bingo. You have not been able to bring the puppy home until she is at least eight weeks old. You and your children are fascinated with this ten-pound bundle of energy and love, and you want to hold, cuddle, play, and just love this little creature with all your might. Young children need to be taught, in fact, that hugging too hard, which seems to be their instinct, can be hurtful to Bingo.

How do you know, and how do you help your children see, when it's time for Bingo to be entertained, when it's time for her to sleep, when it's feeding time, bathing time, and walk time? When is the right time for all those things we need to do to take care of this precious little life? The answer is, we have learned from others who know how to "read" the puppy and how to "listen" to Bingo's behaviors that tell us what she needs. If she's whining and sniffing at her food dish, it's probably sup-pertime. If she's curling up with her eyes drooping—nap time. If she's running around the kitchen like an out-of-control tornado—time to take her for a walk or play catch in the backyard!

These are pretty standard puppy behaviors, and they help us to know how to address Bingo's needs. Each time we correctly interpret Bingo's behaviors and give her what she needs, she knows to do that same behavior again to get the result she needs. She learns to trust that she can give—and we can receive and respond to—the right signals. She comes to trust that the world is a safe place and that we're able to keep her happy and healthy. She belongs to us and we can share in a loving, trusting, relationship.

The big difference between your new baby and Bingo is that by the time Bingo comes home, he is already mobile and has developed some sorts of differentiated behaviors that are recognizable to most of us who have ever been around puppies. This is probably not the case with your baby! Here we have a totally dependent, poorly differentiated little bundle who needs us to interpret every action and anticipate every need, twenty-four hours a day, while not being able to do much of anything except wriggle and cry. If the child is a toddler or older, he may have learned that if he cries out of hunger or fear, he gets kicked, put in a room by himself, or worse yet, ignored. He won't have learned which signals to give in order to get what he needs. Or he may have learned to be cute and superficially charming to get his needs met. If we as parents have no experience, not much self-confidence, and little support from those who have "been there," we can become overwhelmed. We're as confused as the child by his seeming inconsistency of behaviors.

What may further complicate matters is that your adopted child may be from another country and now is probably in sensory overload. Imagine if you were parachuting into a totally foreign culture. You wouldn't know what was happening, and you wouldn't be able to predict what was going to happen next. You would be clueless about language and cultural expectations. And you are an adult—you have already negotiated new and possibly dangerous experiences before! Imagine what it would be like for a child, especially one whose brain has not developed normally. This child has nothing he can use to negotiate his safety or get his needs met, except for the behaviors that get immediate attention or allow release of frustration. This child's experience is based on the experience of being ignored or mistreated and the fear that he won't survive.

Remember, these children live their whole lives on guard against threats and challenges. This keeps them from engaging in healing experiences like being loved, held, and comforted—much less learning about things like consistency and trust. What we need to teach them is self-regulation and acceptance of a trusting, reliable relationship.

One other commonsense piece of advice about "reading" your child comes from a wonderful pediatrician, Bill Hutchison: As much as seems reasonable, expect that your baby will be feeling what you are. If it's cool outside when you take a walk, expect your baby to be as chilly as you are, at least physically. If you need a sweater, so will he. The "reasonable" part is to put yourself in the baby's position. If you were riding in a carriage when it's 35 degrees out, you would need a sweater or jacket, and so will he. If you're jogging while pushing the carriage, you probably won't need the sweater, but put yourself in the baby's position and act accordingly.

What do we see when we have correctly interpreted and met Bingo's needs? Bingo calms herself and exhibits the equivalent of a "puppy smile." We know we have done the right things to make his world safe and to keep him satisfied and happy.

What do we see when we have correctly interpreted and met our baby's needs? See the "Progress" section at the end of the chapter for some clues that attachment is beginning to solidify (and see the list of universal attachment behaviors in chapter 3).

TEACHING SOCIAL CUES

Because of their neurological miswiring, and conditioning, children with attachment problems have difficulty reading body language and facial cues; they have trouble figuring out what people are trying to tell them. It's important for you to help your child learn to interpret what people's bodies, faces, and tones of voice are "saying." Your child may react in unexpected ways to your own behavior: for instance, your child may laugh when you are angry or may seem threatened when you are trying to comfort her. Don't take it personally; rather, explain to the child what your behavior means.

One activity that can help is to show your child pictures of animals or people and make up stories about what is happening to them based on what we can infer from their appearance, posture, and facial expression. What is happening to this person or animal? What behavior can we expect from him or her (i.e., what might happen next?) Helping your child read these important social cues is another opportunity for you to promote attachment.

One parent had this experience:

My daughter is four and for a long time didn't quite "get" who she could be affectionate with and who deserved a handshake or less. We took a long sheet of paper and drew a big heart on one end and drew pictures of our immediate family within it. This was our "family circle of love," and we discussed how we can always act lovingly toward anyone in that circle. [Hint: draw your daughter's birth mother in there too!] Then, in smaller descending hearts we drew extended family members, then friends, then doctors, mail carriers, casual babysitters, and so on. We talked about appropriate behavior for her toward each group and practiced scenarios. I also gave her permission to not hug and kiss anyone outside her immediate family.

ACTIVITIES TO ENHANCE ATTACHMENT

The early weeks with a child may be the best time to initiate some activities that will strongly support the attachment process. Look back at the various lists and descriptions of principles and foundations of attachment. Understanding the underlying principles—the *why* of what you are doing—will help you to expand and adapt any examples in the book to what is most comfortable to you, your child, and your family.

Most of the activities included here should be offered by way of "discoveries" and then facts of which you are very proud. They are designed to bring you and your child closer, feeling as if you belong together, not by accident but by design. So you "discover" things that are similar or the same about you both, and then you proudly announce them to everyone. It's simple and fun. In the process, your child will become convinced that she truly was meant to belong to you, and you to her.

Use these activities (and the ones you add) as often as you can. In addition, make a point of telling your child, and everyone who will stand still long enough to listen, that you are doing them. Sound hokey? After all, your child may not even understand English, right? But think about this. Even though we know that babies don't understand the words of language until months and months after they're born, we still chatter away at them, often explaining in quite animated and sophisticated paragraphs what we're doing, thinking, and feeling. It's part of communicating with our children; they learn the pitch and cadence of our voice, the emotional content of it, and begin to understand what it means.

So even just speaking to your new child is a way to enhance attachment as she learns the words and sounds associated with you. Being spoken to and having positive attention lavished on her are probably new experiences for her. And, of course, this is also a great language-learning experience for your child.

Once the first days of homecoming are over, begin the following types of activities. Play "show and tell" with your baby and anyone else listening, and make sure your family and friends do lots of "oohing" and "aahing" over how great these amazing discoveries are! Two great sources of information about how and why we do these activities are "Theraplay for Adopted Children" (Lindaman 1996) and *I Love You Rituals* (Bailey 2000).

Nicknames

Choose a loving nickname for your child, one that reflects something accurate about her ("Button Nose," "Bright Eyes") or the way you feel about her ("My Heart," "My Little Love") or whatever works for you two. Use it consistently, along with her name. Use it enough that when others who know you think of her, they think of her name and your nickname for her almost at the same time. However, reserve this nickname for you and only the closest people to her.

Similarity Finding

Be alike, any way you can. "Oh, look, little one! We're both wearing the same colors/same type of shirt/same kind of sneakers!" "Our eyes look the same color today!" "We have the same number of toes!" (Then count them, both on you and on your child.) Expand this game to include not just the ways you are alike, but things you do alike. "Look, we wiggle our fingers the same way when we wave bye-bye!" or "Our smiles are the same" (then show her in the mirror). Are you stretching the truth? Be as realistic as possible. But, if it helps your child make the critically important transition from one mother to another, and from one culture to another, then isn't it worth a stretch? You can make charts or pictures of the ways that your family members are alike and post them on the refrigerator, living room, and bedroom. This will be a constant reminder that she is not alone, but part of a bigger whole—a family where she belongs, and in which she is a real, true, honest-to-goodness, and Forever member.

Routine

Establish a routine that works, both for your child and you/your family, and stick to it. Current research in the development of attachment and the brains of children with attachment disorder or difficulties strongly suggests that it is more important that you simply follow a routine than that you spend a certain amount of time on the routine, or complete each part of it.

Your routine in the morning may include waking to cuddle time and a bottle, breakfast, cleanup after breakfast, playtime, reading, a snack together, and then nap. Normally, you have a regular amount of time you spend on each activity, until you reach that golden activity, naptime. One day you may be in a hurry to get your child into bed for her nap. Don't skip reading (or playtime or snack together) as your solution. Instead, spend a little less time playing, then a little less time reading, and a bit less snack time. That way, your child will have engaged in all pieces of the routine she has come to regard as necessary, even though each one may not have been as long as usual. Do each piece of the routine in order, regardless of the time. She will miss the actual piece of the routine more than she will be aware that the time you spend on each piece is different.

Baby Games

Play baby games as part of your regular day. If you were able to learn some games from your child's homeland or early environment, use them exclusively in the beginning, then gradually interweave your own into the mix, eventually (but what's the hurry?) changing over to those you learned as a child. If you were not fortunate enough to learn some baby games native to your child, use the ones with which you are most familiar and comfortable. Start with the most simple and infant ones. Keep doing them whenever you have the chance. Play them and play them and play them, until you are sick of them. Even if your child gives you every indication that *she* too is sick of them, do them more and more and more.

Here's why. Think back to the beginning of this chapter and to the principles of attachment. Children who are afraid of attachment (to some degree, most internationally adopted and certainly all neglected ones) will resist attachment activities when they begin to actually "take hold." When you think they are telling you, "Back off!" they are actually telling you, "I'm afraid, but I think this is something I need, so please teach me that attaching to you is a safe thing. Do some more."

Playing games can also help your child begin to read social cues: when someone smiles, or frowns, or has a questioning look, what does that mean? Try to incorporate games with lots of facial expressions into your regular playtime. Name the feeling that goes with the face, so helping your child learn the association.

These "baby games" should be continued throughout childhood and even into adolescence. Children with attachment difficulties will not "outgrow" the need for these games. In my practice I have seen tough teenagers who, after initial reluctance, are more than willing to play peekaboo with me because on a deep profound level they know they need this type of stimulation and reconnection with their injured core. They respond to games like these because they did not get the chance to play them as children, and this deprivation created holes in their development. Why are games like peekaboo and hide-and-seek universal? Because they are vital to healthy neurological development. Even if your school-age child knows perfectly well that you are hiding behind the sofa (perhaps your feet are sticking out) or that he is visible under the blanket on his bed, the process of "seeking" each other, over and over again, is what is important here. I tell all parents *always* to focus on their child's emotional level rather than his or her chronological age. Remember that, for the most part, children who come to us with any type of attachment difficulties are emotionally young compared with their chronological age.

Team Building

Call yourselves a team, always, and mean it. This child can't make the transition by herself. She must be part of a team—with you— to attach and emotionally survive and ultimately truly belong to you. During games that involve the whole family, especially in the beginning, you must be the child's team member. Whether you win or lose makes little difference. The fact that you two (or three or four) are on the same team, and that you win or lose graciously but together, is what counts. Always congratulate her, even if she hasn't played very hard; she is learning something very new (being part of a team), and this is the most difficult "game" of all.

What to do if she won't play on your team? I suggest you explain to the other players that your teammate simply isn't ready at this point to participate. You may express regret that this is so, but try not to be angry—just accept it. However, she must stay in the room with you and is not allowed to watch television, play Game Boy, or otherwise disengage from your family activity. She sits on the sidelines and watches. Or maybe serves as referee. This is appropriate, at least in the beginning. If you sense she really wants to participate but is afraid, you might have her play on your shoulders or hold her on your hip. If, after months and many opportunities, she persists in staying separate, you may wish to talk with a professional about other ideas of how to integrate her more into playtime activities with your family.

Positive Talk

Spend energy turning negatives into positives. For example, if your child is a "nagger" (or, in other words, doesn't give up), keep an even temper and compliment her on how persistent she is—a virtue, of course. And then you can teach her that "patience is also a virtue." I know, it's easier said than done. But parents report that if they try hard to change their attitude about their child's less-than-pleasant traits, their child's behavior often changes for the better (after an initial thrashing around by your child when the old patterns don't work anymore). The secret here, I believe, is that you have to be convinced that this child is not doing these things or being this way to spite you, but rather because these are habits ingrained in her young neurology or driven by fear. Be happy there is still time to reverse the pattern, and then go for it!

Tease-Free Zone

Don't tease. Developing trust is the most critical piece of the attachment process. Teasing may seem like fun and may be cause for giggles and laughter. But try to imagine how you would feel being teased by someone you don't know very well or haven't learned to trust, especially because you're not sure if the thing you're being teased about is true. That's how your child will feel.

Naming Parts

Tell her often about the fascinating and lovable "parts" of her. "Look how beautifully brown your eyes are today! They have sparkles in them!" "However did your skin become absolutely velvety this morning? I could touch it forever!" Even things that are expected, such as having the same number of fingers, toes, and ears from one day to the next, are cause for delighted comments: "Oh, wonderful! You brought those adorable little toes with you—the ones I love to wiggle!" and then actually wiggle or even kiss them. We do this with babies all the time, and it helps them believe they are truly lovable creatures, right down to their toes!

OVERCOMING NEGATIVE SELF-IMAGE

Children with attachment problems have come to believe that their bodies, and the feelings inside them, are not very lovable; some even believe they are deep down, irrevocably, awfully ugly and unlovable. If you tell them you love them, your words, no matter how heartfelt and true, cause confusion in their little underdeveloped cognition. The psychological phenomenon called *cognitive dissonance* states that we cannot hold two contradictory beliefs in our mind at the same time. So, if I believe I'm unlovable, and you tell me you love me, I'm in a dilemma. What happens in these instances is that the child has to continue to believe one of those things and discount the other. In doing so, she also has to discount the person who tells her those uncomfortable, unbelievable things that contradict what she has come to hold true.

Imagine, for example, that I compliment you enthusiastically on your "terrific blue hair." You know you don't have blue hair. Therefore, you have no choice but to discount, or not believe, what I am telling you, and you come not to trust me because I am telling you this unbelievable thing. In other words, you come to believe that I am a liar, or at best color-blind. Either way, you're going to be very suspicious of most everything else I tell you from now on. What a sad state of affairs between a new parent and child.

One good way to help establish a new self-concept without dealing head-on with this cognitive dissonance is explained by Greg Keck and Regina Kupecky in their book, *Parenting the Hurt Child* (2002). They suggest that "sometimes it is good for hurt children to overhear praise instead of receiving it directly. This methodology is less threatening and can have a positive effect. A parent can call a friend—or simply dial up the weather recording—and talk about something that the child did well. The hypervigilance of most hurt children almost guarantees that they'll hear every conversation."

What else can you do to counter this "unlovable" self-image? You can use a process of systematic desensitization. Point out small, true, and positives things about your child, regularly and in a matter-of-fact manner. Catch the child being good and point that out to her. Compliment her, even about the smallest trait or deed. Just make sure that you do it honestly; otherwise, you will stir up mistrust again. Here is one instance where you want to be careful to be very accurate. Don't tell her she's the best artist in the class if she's not. But do find something that is true about her drawings that you—and others—can honestly commend (e.g., "You use more colors in your pictures than anyone else in your play group!"), and say it with a smile so she knows you see this as a positive thing.

DEALING WITH TEMPORARY SEPARATIONS

As hard as we try, there are times when you simply have to leave your child alone, if only for a few hours or overnight. This can be a stressful time in the life of a child with attachment issues. For many children the most difficult period of experiencing separation is when they are actually in the healing process and have begun to experience both the joys and the inevitable vulnerability of feeling attached to a safe person who returns that love.

I hope that for the sake of both you and your child that you do not have to be apart often. But for those times that you do, here are some ways to help your child through the inevitable separations. These can easily be amended to fit a situation in which your child is the one who has to be away.

- Allow your child to sleep with your pillow while you are away. You may even want to let the child sleep in your bed in your absence.
- Wear your own favorite tee-shirt or sleepwear and then leave it for your child to wear to bed or when he or she misses you. Don't wash the shirt after wearing it! It will smell like you, and that is a great part of the "magic."
- Take a picture of your child with you (either a photo or a drawing), and make sure he knows you will keep the picture close to you. Make a drawing for him, although be aware that he may "lose" it if he's angry at some point of being separated from you.
- Prepare notes or "secret messages" for your child to open while you're away. Emphasize that you are thinking of her at the very moment she is reading it. Say that you miss her as much as she misses you.
- Decide ahead of time when you will be able to phone your child. Make sure your caregiver knows when that time will be so the child doesn't miss the call.
- Make sure your child's caregiver is aware of the problems that can be stirred up by your absence. Distraction can help an emotionally upset child; the caregiver can take the child to a favorite place, restaurant, or the library or can read a favorite book endless times.
- Plan a celebration to mark your return. It should be quiet, without too many people around, and should focus on attachment-type activities—ones that we've described or those that you have already found are soothing for your child.

If you leave your child at a babysitter's house or at a day-care center, remember that he will have pent-up frustrations and fear from the entire day. When you arrive at the end of your time away, and *before you leave* the sitter's home, day-care center, or place your child has been staying, let the child process those feelings. Reassure him that you are back. Hold him, sit with him, let him spend five, ten, fifteen minutes working through reconnecting. Apologize for having left him but explain that you will never leave him for more time than he can handle. This should *not* be "putting on your coat, gathering up your things" time, but quiet time when you can sit, relaxed, hold each other, and look into his eyes as he lets you know he is angry at your leaving him. It really works, sometimes not in five minutes in the beginning, but he learns how to sort of throw his worry and anger out in his "trash can" at the door, leaving his anxiety there. The two of you can then go home together in a happy, connected spirit.

PROGRESS

It is always an exciting day for me in therapy when a formerly unattached or perhaps avoidantly/anxiously attached mother/child team comes into my office and Mom complains about something very different from when I first met her: "It used to hurt my feelings when Marty would go to anyone and seem to not even care if I was in the room. Now I can't even go to the bathroom without Marty crying outside the bathroom door to let him in!" Mom may be annoyed at this turn of events, but as momentarily upsetting as it may be, we both know it is a triumph.

I can be sympathetic with Mom's need for a bit of time to herself, but much more so I rejoice that Marty is finally developing a sense of belonging, of not wanting to be without Mom. This is what should happen in the natural course of events between mother and child. It is a healthy, recognizable developmental stage. It is an integral part of the process of attaching, of belonging. It is a temporary stage, to be sure, and Mom needs and deserves the reassurance that it will be intense until Marty has internalized the sense that he belongs to Mom, as she to him, whether or not she is in the room with him at that moment. But it is a critical rung up the ladder of attachment, of mental well-being for the child, and of stability in the relationship between mother and child, and later between the child and future attachment figures.

How will you know when your baby is starting to attach to you? Here is what Dr. Goff has to say:

You will feel this intuitively, but there are specific behaviors you can watch for. As your baby attaches to you she will make increasing eye contact, be more comfortable being held, snuggle herself against you, start to seek comfort from you. She may start to touch your face, stick her fingers in your mouth, or want to feed you pieces of food at the table. She will babble at you more and smile socially at you. Depending on her developmental level, she may start to show anxiety when you go out of sight and not want to be held by others. This last sign of attachment can be extreme in some children who have been in foster care. Although this separation anxiety can complicate your life (going to the bathroom, taking showers), it is a wonderfully positive sign. No wonder she is anxious: she has decided to jump into your lifeboat!

ABOUT LIZ

Liz is a five-year-old adopted from China whose Mom had this to say about her development after beginning therapy:

Life with Liz has been very interesting since our last visit with you. Seems to have provided a small breakthrough for her. She was extremely quiet on the way home. Part of that was that she was exhausted and slept much of the way. But when she wasn't asleep she hardly made a peep. She asked for a story, listened without interrupting (amazing) and spoke calmly when she did talk to me. We went home and had supper with Bob [Dad] and then went out for ice cream. She was snuggly and kept saying "I love you" and kissing me. She was pretty peaceful for the whole evening, and after she went to bed Bob commented that he thought he was seeing the "real" Liz.

She invented a game that she asks to play with me several times a day every day. It's the "Baby Liz" game and the script is something like this: "Mama, pretend you meet a Chinese lady." The Chinese lady (Liz) tells me to come with her; she has something to show me. "Mama, pretend you see a little baby. Be surprised because the baby wants you to be her Mama. Be surprised that she loves you already and wants to come home with you." Then she will snuggle into my lap and make the cutest little baby noises. Liz often tells me that there are two Lizzes and that I brought the big Liz and the baby Liz home and that the Big Liz can tell me what the Little Liz is saying.

When we play this game I can get away with saying anything, so I tell her that she is such a good, beautiful, smart baby and that I am so lucky to have her and that we will be a family forever. The game has deteriorated only very slightly since we started last week. She seems to be able to take a lot more love when she plays this—although this morning we played, and then when we were done she said, "Don't love me so much!"

She has also been much more willing to talk about how she feels and will even do so without being asked first. She has also played a game where we have to adopt her stuffed animals a lot this week. . . .

We've had a very good couple of weeks with Liz. She's already doing a bit better with the speaking loud enough to be heard. Though I think she still needs work both in the control and shame departments, her teacher has already noticed an improvement. These last couple of weeks I have been working hard at not letting Liz manipulate me into talking for her. Believe it or not, Bob and I still have to work hard at not saying "Okay?" after everything we say to Liz, but we're still working at that, too.

Anyway, had a few really nice things happen. One day Liz was not feeling too happy and she asked me for bottle time. We had a very nice one that did not need to deteriorate into holding time. The best moment recently was Sunday afternoon. Liz was supposed to bring some pretty leaves into school for a project, and we needed groceries, so Bob and I agreed that he would do the leaves and I would do the store. Bob and Liz went outside to start looking and I got in the car. I was backing out of the driveway and Liz came running up to me and gave me a big wet kiss and then ran back to Daddy and happily grabbed his hand so that they could go off and do their thing. Sigh! It was one of those great moments when I thought, "Yeah! This is how it's supposed to be!" We also had a great time this Saturday. Bob and I were to provide music for a weekend retreat. When we were singing, Liz peacefully drew pictures. When we weren't, we were either playing together on the playground or snuggling really nicely in the cabin. AMAZING. I couldn't believe how great a time we had.

One more event I should share relates to her handling of the shame "I don't want you to tell me I'm good" thing. Last Sunday after Sunday school she said to me, "Mom, I want to tell you something but I'm too embarrassed." She was visibly upset about this conflict. So I sat her down and hugged her on my lap right there in the hallway and said, "It's okay, Liz, you can tell me anything." "Okay," she replied, "I'll tell you, but just don't tell me I'm good." (Usually if I do, she gets physically agitated and whiny.) So I promised. [Remember the *cognitive dissonance* discussed earlier?] She said to me, "Today Meredith [a girl in Sunday school] said she was cold and I gave her my coat to wear. Now don't tell me I'm good!!" Usually I would have said something like, "That's great, Liz! You were being a really good friend!" But this time I just said, "Liz, I'm really glad you told me." That was that. She was fine, and we went on with our day.

III

COPING WITH
ATTACHMENT
DISORDERS

HEALTH CARE: MEDICAL PROBLEMS FROM AN ATTACHMENT PERSPECTIVE

Just because your country of origin has a low rate of incidence of a certain malady (in China, fewer HIV/AIDS and drug-dependent babies) does not mean they are home free. Parents that adopt should know that the world has an equal distribution of problems, so do not be misled that your child is healthy. . . . Help your physician become aware of the situation. Here is a situation, perhaps the first of many, where you have to be an advocate for your child.

—MOTHER OF TWO CHILDREN ADOPTED FROM CHINA

Children who are adopted from neglectful environments or underdeveloped countries often bring medical problems with them, adding another stressor to the hugely important transition from the orphanage or foster care setting to the home of their Forever Family.

Some medical problems may be obvious, but others are hidden. Orphanage personnel have been known to give a sick child the "all-clear." Some orphanages are so understaffed, or the conditions so primitive, that medical problems may be chronic or misunderstood. Some conditions such as malnourishment, skin diseases, or worms may be endemic in the child's native country. Even after your child is living with you, medical problems may be hidden, often for long periods of time, because the medical personnel in our country cannot be trained in every possible medical problems from any and every backround and far-flung part of the globe. They may not be aware of what it is they should try to seek out or identify.

Chronic stress also affects the body's immune system, so adopted children may be at risk for such disorders as allergies, asthma, eczema, or seborrhea. In chapter 5 we discussed environmental measures you can take to help ameliorate some of these conditions.

Make an appointment to see a pediatrician as soon as possible after the child arrives. Some families have gone so far as to bring their pediatrician with them or to have the pediatrician conduct an examination of the child through real-time Internet access. The child may not have had the usual inoculations for a child his age; make sure he gets them.

Getting medical care for your child is another opportunity to promote attachment. Handling medical problems in a confident, consistent manner conveys to the child that you are in charge and will take care of him and keep him safe. If your child must undergo a painful medical procedure, make sure the child associates the pain with the doctor or nurse, not with you, the parents.

What seems to us a benign experience such as going to the doctor may trigger painful memories for your child. Do not be embarrassed. Stay very attentive, sympathetic, and physically close to your child, even lying down on the examining table with your child, holding and comforting him as you would an infant. Remember, focus on the child's emotional age, not his chronological age, and pay attention to any cues he may give you that he is afraid or more tense than usual. You should reassure the child that you have faith in the medical personnel who are attending to him. If you don't have confidence, you probably won't stay and most likely won't go back. Remember, your job is to protect and advocate for your child.

EDUCATING THE PHYSICIAN

Some physicians here in the United States remain ignorant about the medical and psychological conditions that can afflict internationally adopted children. "The standard advice about sleeping, feeding, discipline and catching-up is all opposite," says Dr. Goff. And the medical conditions can vary from one country of origin to another. For example, Dr. Goff has found that children adopted from China are fairly healthy—at least physically. They are usually well nourished, but 10 to 20 percent have scabies or eczema. The children do get exercise, and their fine and gross motor skills are satisfactory. "They catch up pretty well," she said. "Most are fairly well attached." Her experience has found that Guatemalan children for the most part, too, are well nourished, usually in foster care, and well attached.

The situation is different in Russia. Many Russian orphans are malnourished and have serious developmental delays. In Romania as well, most orphans are not normally attached. Children from Vietnam and Cambodia vary in their health status.

THE IDEAL DOCTOR FOR AN ADOPTED CHILD

Gary Flanders, a therapeutic parent from Colorado, offers the following picture of an ideal medical professional for a child with attachment difficulties. An ideal professional is someone who will

- Believe the child's mother and will ask Mom before believing what the child says
- Be open to the concept that severe neglect in early life can have lasting if not permanent emotional effects on a child
- Understand the importance of the first few years of a child's life, in terms of that child's ability to relate to other authority figures in his or her life
- Support the parents in their efforts to provide a suitable environment in which the child feels safe, even in the medical setting and even if it conflicts with usual office procedures
- Understand that not all children are the same and thus should not be parented and medically treated the same, even if this situation feels odd at first
- Be courageous enough to resist automatically prescribing common medications (e.g., Ritalin) and be open to looking at alternative medications or emotional therapy

Start searching for such a doctor early on, and don't be afraid to ask questions of the physicians you contact. A positive experience with the doctor will provide your child further evidence that you're taking care of him and ensuring his well-being.

INSURANCE

Insurance coverage can be a huge problem for children with attachment problems who need extensive psychological and psychiatric treatment. Susan, the mother of Mike, the adopted boy from Romania about whom you read in chapter 4, pulls no punches when describing the hurdles she faced while persuading insurance companies to pay for her son's treatment:

> If you don't persevere, they will give you squat. They make it as difficult as possible in hopes you will give up. You have to shout the loudest and make them uncomfortable. Eventually they see you know what you're talking about and you're not going to give up.
>
> If you expect your child to be serviced in an appropriate way, forget it; you'll have to fight for you child. No one will give you anything unless you're willing to do battle, literally. It used to be that I'd ask, try to persuade. Now I plan to go in with my guns blazing. I have my argument planned out before I even make the first phone call.
>
> Regarding the insurance system, I started learning how to play the game and make threats: "If my son hurts himself or hurts me, I'm going to sue you." I would tell them that I would call the attorney general, and I did. I would tell them that if they didn't provide for my son's mental health needs by providing for a mental health professional who is knowledgeable in his disorder, I would call the mental health advocacy association, and I did. When they say, "No," you say, "that's not acceptable."
>
> You have to be willing to call day after day after day, and you have to track it. I write down who I talked to, when I

called, and a summary of what's been said. It's a constant battle of being on the phone and keeping track of what they pay and what they don't. You can't assume that they're going to pay for things, even if they say they're going to. You have to stay on top of the paperwork.

I write down every call. You're always looking to build your case. They keep tapes of their calls "for quality assurance." If there's a dispute, you can say, "if you check your own tapes…" You use all those pieces of information.

Early on I got fed up with talking to "Joe Blow," and I insisted on talking to supervisors. I bypassed the whole group of people who knew nothing and I got to the people who could clear us for services. We spent tremendous amounts of money before I figured out how to play the game.

You want to have a primary contact person; you don't want to be talking to a different person every time. With one contact person, I didn't have to worry about getting different stories.

At one point this mother's insurance company wanted to know exactly how many times a week her son was hitting her; this apparently was the basis on which they were making decisions about whether or not to authorize treatment. Here is a copy of a letter that another frustrated adoptive parent sent to his insurance company:

I don't know if you are aware of it, but since your decision to abruptly (with less than 24 hours' notice) discontinue my son David's therapy with a specialist, David has experienced a severe setback, not a surprise to anyone familiar with his care. Last Monday, upset that therapy had been cancelled, he had a blowout fight with his therapeutic foster parent, Mr. C. David ran away from home and accused Mr. C of physically abusing him. He is currently in a respite home while the situation is sorted out.

It is very frustrating to see the effort that David, my wife, and I have invested in this therapy be wasted. For a little over a year now, I have taken off work and my wife has rearranged her busy schedule to attend therapy. We are willing to make this sacrificial commitment for one very good reason: IT IS WORKING. For twelve years, David has seen over fifty therapists. Not one has made a lasting impact, until this specialist. It has been our experience that most therapists, psychologists and psychiatrists don't have a clue about attachment disorder or how to treat it. Making matters worse, they usually refuse to acknowledge that they don't know what they are dealing with or how to treat it.

We believe your decision to disrupt appropriate therapy has jeopardized David's healing process and we appeal to you to reconsider before further damage is done. Without good attachment and trauma treatment, it is likely that David will end up back in a residential treatment facility, which will cost your company more money. Whether you acknowledge it or not, it was directly due to the progress David made under therapy that allowed him to be moved from a residential treatment facility to a therapeutic foster home last spring. Already that has saved you thousands of dollars.

Finally, upon being notified at 4:45 p.m. Friday evening that the therapist's services were being discontinued for David the next day, my wife requested a grievance filing. I am requesting that we skip any internal grievance proceedings and go directly to a second-level grievance. It has been our experience in the past that internal grievances merely function as a stall tactic and serve only to delay the second level. My son can't afford the wait.

I would appreciate your prompt response. For your information we have also initiated a grievance with the Department of Public Welfare.

This father also sent copies of this letter to the county mental health/mental retardation office, the state Health Law Project, the Office of Managed Behavioral Healthcare, the state attorney general's office, and the State Mental Health Consumers Association.

9

SCHOOL: HOW TO
MAKE IT POSITIVE IN
YOUR CHILD'S LIFE

*As far as the school system goes, you're probably not going to get a lot
of help. In my son's situation, it was true that the principal didn't
want to be bothered with a special needs child, but this is not true
with all schools: in the district where I work we bend over backward
to help these children. But most times the school will know nothing
about these disorders. You need to bring in a professional to educate
them. I always give them books, pamphlets, copies of psychiatric
reports to help them understand.*

—SUSAN, SCHOOL COUNSELOR AND MOTHER
OF MIKE, A BOY ADOPTED FROM ROMANIA

We will talk in this chapter about the kind of structure that children
with attachment disorders need in school and strategies that can
help these children succeed. We will also stress school districts' obligations

to provide services for the children who need them and how to overcome the roadblocks that school districts all too often put in the way of parents seeking the educational services to which their child is entitled.

I used to be an elementary school principal. For ten wonderful years I worked with children and their families, teachers, and the extended community to produce, as best we could, the healthiest and most positive stimulation for young children in their earliest formal education setting. It was an exhilarating and emotionally satisfying experience, and I loved it. It also made me realize how much extra support some children need and how much schools need to learn about meeting those needs.

SELF-REGULATION AND THE "TEACHABLE MOMENT"

We've referred to the concept of self-regulation earlier in this book, and it is particularly relevant to schooling. Children with attachment disorders have neurologically based difficulties with self-regulation that make it hard for them to succeed in a classroom setting. Hypervigilance and control issues have replaced trust in caregivers. The child may become frightened if he senses he is losing control of the environment. He may become locked in the states of fight, flight, or freeze. Once this happens, problems with school, poor peer interactions, developmental delays, sensory issues, and even hygiene may follow.

Clancey Blair from the Pennsylvania State University's Department of Human Development and Family Studies wrote the following in an article about the neurological model of the development of self-regulation skills and how it affects school readiness: "Researchers examining self-regulation in adolescence and adulthood have long recognized the relevance of emotional state and emotion-related processes to the functioning of component processes of cognitive regulation. Implications of emotionality for cognitive regulation in young children, in whom brain structures associated with emotionality are developmentally in advance of those associated with higher-order thinking, however, have not really been considered" (Blair 2002). In other words, we understand that emotional self-regulation is critical to academic (cognitive) learning in teenagers and adults. But we forget to take it into consideration with children, when it may be the most critical factor. What we want is for these children to be in the state of "calm alert," ready to learn something new. To use an example from nature, imagine a cat stealthily watching a bird, all parts of her body focused on her prey. For an infant, "calm alert" could mean "talking" with his parents through intense eye contact. For a toddler, it could be the total focus that she devotes to watching her parents use a spoon, in preparation for holding and using one herself. Picture a slightly older child as he waits for his piece of cake to be cut at his birthday party. There is all kinds of noise, wiggling, and giggling around him, but he knows that it is *his* piece of cake being cut and he watches like a hawk to make sure that not one crumb is dropped on the way to his plate. He is totally focused.

We are describing a "teachable moment," those few precious seconds when you have the intense and undivided attention—actually the thirst—of every child in the class. They are focused on you and the pearls of wisdom you are about to impart to them. You are the magician, about to perform magic, and they want to see and believe.

ENHANCING TEACHING FOR CHILDREN WITH ATTACHMENT ISSUES

Unfortunately, for children with persistent and pervasive attachment problems, this focused state is both very difficult to find and next to impossible to maintain. Whether the child has average, below-average, or above-average intelligence, emotional issues can prevent her from using her potential as a learner. Because of this, emotional and behavioral considerations *must* take priority over academics. The child may require a special aide for emotional and behavioral support during class time, lunch, or recess.

Self-regulation—being able to release anxiety, tension, and hyper-vigilance—is critical to learning, so it should be the primary focus. School learning, and certainly grades, became secondary until the ability to focus, concentrate, process, and integrate information is reached and strengthened. Once your child reaches that healthier state of being able to learn, then she can be more successful in what we consider to be traditional learning.

Children spend many hours a day in school, and the school environment should match, as much as possible, that at home. The school should be aware of the child's problems and ideally reinforce and support the measures the parents are taking to solve them. There should be as much stability and consistency as possible in the child's school day, with minimal changes in personnel and routine, just as you, as parents, strive to create a stable, reassuring, consistent routine at home.

You will most likely need to help schools understand how best to help your child. "Funneling" is one process that teachers can use to minimize the distance between the child's home life and school life. Instead of saying, "I'm proud of you!" the teacher says, "Your mom and dad are so proud of you! Let's make sure they know what a great job you've done!" Likewise, if the child is having difficulty following rules or completing assignments, the teacher might say, "Mom and Dad would not be proud of what you're doing. How would they help you deal with this situation?"

The teacher may be reluctant to use the "funneling" technique, arguing that it would be awkward to say "I am proud" of one child and "Mom and Dad are proud" of another. I suggest using the latter for all children.

Here are some examples of "funneling" comments that you might share with your child's teachers. As you can see, they are fine for all children, but you've learned by now that they are critically important for your child:

1. Your mom loves you.
2. Your mom does lots of good things for you.
3. What would your mom think?
4. Would your parents allow you to do that?
5. Save that; I want to show it to your mom.
6. Let me have that. I want to show your mom.
7. Let's take a picture of you for your mom and dad.
8. Do you think I'm the one in charge? Your parents make the schedule.
9. Why do you think your mom does that?
10. I bet your mom would be pleased to know you [action or behavior].

11. Let's call your mom. You can tell her how well you did on this [test, project].
12. Mom must have been thinking of you when . . . (she packed your favorite snack, made sure you had a good eraser, helped you be so healthy, etc.)
13. Takes a mom to solve a problem like that.
14. Sometimes it's tough having a good mom like you do.
15. You make a lot of comments about your mom, but you have to admit . . .
16. Good thing that mom remembered that.
17. You have a great mom to do this for you.

COMMUNICATION BETWEEN HOME AND SCHOOL

When I was a principal I made it a point to communicate with parents *immediately* if there was a problem, and parents knew they could always contact me as well. Communication between home and school is important for all children but especially for children with attachment disorder, many of whom have learned to become expert manipulators. Daily communication between teachers, parents, and aides is essential. Notes may be used for less important matters, but phone calls and conferences are needed for more serious matters. Communication should be between the school and the parents, never using the child as a go-between! The child's goal may be to "triangulate" the adults in his world: if the parents or the school always believe what the child says, without confirmation, the child is in a prime position to manipulate one or both, and he knows it.

You may need to be persistent to make sure that school staff consult with you if they have questions about stories your child tells in school or excuses he gives. The child's therapist can assist, if needed, for clarification. If your child portrays himself as "the poor orphan whom no one loves," the school staff should bring this behavior to your attention. Staff should not overtly sympathize with or pity the student.

Susan, Mike's mother, said she had difficulty communicating with her son's teachers: "I tried to prepare them for the cycles he went through, but the teacher would think I was nuts. Year after year I'd try to warn them about how best to work with my son, but the attitude was, they're the teachers, they know best."

Special education teachers, the guidance counselor, the school nurse, and the school aide must be educated about attachment disorders. A unified team of adults, responding to the child in a consistent fashion, will provide the best environment for the child to heal.

Special education teachers, wraparound personnel (one-to-one aides), the guidance counselor, aides, support staff and resource teachers, and any regular education teachers should meet with the parents on a monthly basis to discuss progress, adjustments, and strategies to assist the child in being more successful in the school environment.

It will be up to you as parents to keep the staff informed of the treatment modalities and interventions being used for the child and to apprise those working closely with your child about issues being handled in therapy.

Once again, be sure the consistent, overarching emphasis is on your role as parents. Neither the school nor the staff is to provide for the child; all good things must come from the parents. The parents must be portrayed as the ones with ultimate authority and control. Staff can provide explanation and reinforcement for the parents' actions: "Of course your mom said 'no.' What kind of mom would let a child who can't take a bath go out with friends? They would laugh at him and call him names."

Likewise, staff should not answer questions that the parents should answer: "I know the answer to that, but normal, healthy kids get that information from their mother. Aren't you lucky you have one now?"

Many of the families with whom I've worked have chosen to home-school. Many have found this to be an exceptionally good choice for their family, at least during the child's attachment process.

THE IDEAL TEACHER

Therapeutic foster parent Gary Flanders has come up with a list of qualities that characterize the ideal teacher for a child with attachment disorder. Children with attachment disorders tend to need these things:

- A tight, loving structure
- A person who says what they mean and means what they say
- Someone who will check out all the facts and not give a child the benefit of the doubt
- Someone who will not be easily manipulated by a child who desperately tries to be in control of all adult interactions
- Someone who understands that academic considerations must take a back seat when a child needs to "pass life" before he can "pass classes"
- Someone who knows that there is a reason why my child is doing the things he is doing but that until he stops acting out, he will have a very sad life
- Someone who realizes that my child can be superficially charming to an adult with whom he does not have to be in an intimate (family) relationship (e.g., teacher)
- Someone who will not prejudge my parenting without asking me why I do certain things with my child
- Someone who will be a strong person so my child can feel safe and can go back to being a baby in his or her company

POTENTIAL PROBLEMS IN SCHOOL— AND PREVENTING THEM

All adults working with your child, just like you as parents, must realize that an attachment-impaired child's social and emotional development is delayed and not congruent with his chronological age. The child will display these delays inconsistently: for instance, immature behaviors typical of a younger child at one point in the day but more age-appropriate behaviors later in the day. On lower-functioning days, teaching may need to be more individualized, using techniques suitable for younger children.

For the child with an attachment disorder, survival has depended on his ability to control his environment. Staff should anticipate that control battles may well take place in school and should plan interventions ahead of time. Adults in charge should not challenge the child if they can't be sure of winning.

You can help school personnel be prepared for the child's emotional response of fight, flight, or freeze. Even minor frustrations or fear of failure, coupled with the child's history of trauma, can easily trigger the child to react emotionally. Help the school plan tactics for dealing with these occurrences, so aggression, truancy, and dissociation do not result and cause your child more frustration and embarrassment.

The idea is to help your child calm down—to teach him self-soothing as part of self-regulation. *Self-soothing* can be one of many types of activities that are relaxing, repetitive, or comforting and that will help return the child to a calm state. You may suggest that the school provide a place (with supervision!) for your child to do one of these activities to help him regain self-control:

- Rocking in a rocking chair
- Swinging
- Spinning on a tire swing
- Doing jumping jacks
- Doing push-ups
- Jumping on a trampoline
- Blowing bubbles
- Running up and down the stairs
- Holding a fuzzy blanket or personal item
- Imagining a safe place
- Doing art projects (clay, Play-Doh)
- Wearing a *weighted vest* (may be placed on the child's lap)
- Cuddling in a soft or fuzzy blanket

The child should never be left alone; he should always have adult supervision. Even a solo walk home from the bus stop can present problems, so parents may need to provide transportation to and from school.

If your child is prone to self-injury, the school nurse should be part of the therapeutic team and should consult with you and your child's therapist. Staff members must know the correct response should self-injury occur.

Your child may need more time to complete homework on days when he has sessions with his therapist. You should communicate this information directly to the teacher; don't even ask or ever allow your child to be the intermediary.

The child may need to take tests in the emotional or learning support classroom, where there are fewer distractions. Close supervision is advisable if cheating has been a problem. Like other students, he may receive assistance in understanding a question if he respectfully asks for help.

Some children try hard to keep people physically and emotionally distant, often by having poor manners and poor hygiene. It's helpful to use natural consequences to help solve the problem, but the behavior must be identified for your child. You may have to help school staff understand this, so they don't think this is how you choose your child to be. Teachers can help your child understand natural consequences (e.g., "It's pretty clear that your friends don't want to play with you today because you smell so bad; perhaps tomorrow if you come to school clean, your friends will be happy for you to play with them again").

Stealing may be an issue. Parents and staff should eliminate, as much as possible, the chance that items can be either lost or found. The parents may need to provide a list of the child's possessions at school.

You and school personnel should agree on rules that are clear to your child. Then, don't give him more than one warning for inappropriate behavior. If he does not heed the warning, there are no second chances. A calm, matter-of-fact delivery of appropriate consequences should follow immediately.

Paradoxically, success in the classroom can be a problem. If your child's internal picture of himself is negative, success will be uncomfortable to him, possibly resulting in behavior problems. Help staff understand that they should avoid making generalized statements such as "good job," "nice work," or "wonderful student." Instead, refer back to the list of attachment-supporting statements preseated earlier.

IEPs

An individualized education program (IEP) is a document required of all U.S. school districts for special needs students. The IEP lists, in specific detail, the needs of the child and states the school's obligations to the child. Susan, Mike's mother, ended up writing a suggested IEP for her son "because I had more information than anyone about him than anyone else."

Here is part of an IEP that I helped to prepare for a girl named Brandi. Brandi was a badly abused infant and toddler; with her brother, she was locked in a dark basement with her mother's pet rats and snakes. The child was placed with three consecutive preadoptive families, then sent at age seven to a residential placement facility before finally being adopted. This IEP reflects several of the basic tenets of addressing attachment disorders and involves many of the above techniques that are key to helping children with RAD. Reading Brandi's school requirements may help you with some ideas you can consider for your child:

1. Brandi needs to have a one-to-one aide for emotional and behavioral support, at least during less structured situations, including lunch. This person must be within eyesight and earshot of Brandi at all times. This need may be met through wraparound services.

2. Emotional and behavioral considerations must take priority over academics.

3. All adults working with Brandi need to realize that her social and emotional development is years behind her chronological age. Brandi is a child who experienced emotional trauma at several different stages of her development. She has not been able to resolve those traumas until now, as she has not been in a stable environment with parents she can trust. She is just now learning that her parents will not "throw me away" (to use her words) if she shares her early damage. Brandi feels responsible for the things that happened to her and is quite ashamed that she must have been so awful to have brought these abusive acts on herself.

4. Special education teachers, the guidance counselor, the school nurse, and Brandi's one-to-one aide need to have some basic education about reactive attachment disorder and post-traumatic stress disorder. Parents are happy to suggest references and resources.

5. All adults working with Brandi need to realize that she will tend to respond with "fight, flight, or freeze" to even seemingly minor frustrations or stressors and that this response is physiological (related to brain chemistry and development).

6. If Brandi becomes overly anxious or is responding with "fight, flight, or freeze," she needs a time-out before returning to schoolwork. This time-out can be simply allowing her to put her head down on her desk to regroup or may be taking a walk with her one-to-one aide or going (with the supervision of her one-to-one aide) to the emotional support or learning support classroom to regroup. Brandi still needs to be responsible for work she misses during time-outs.

7. "Funneling" Brandi's emotional needs back to her parents is an important way to encourage conscience development and attachment.

8. Daily communication between teachers and parents and between the one-to-one aide and parents is essential, for example, through notes written in a notebook or phone calls regarding more serious matters. Parents, not Brandi, will communicate any and all messages from home. Likewise, all messages from school to home must be in writing or over the phone, not conveyed verbally through Brandi.

9. As long as Brandi is clear about the rules, she should never be given more than one warning for inappropriate behavior. If unheeded, this warning should be followed quickly with a calm, matter-of-fact delivery of appropriate consequences.

10. Due to her diagnosis of attention deficit hyperactivity disorder, Brandi needs a minimum of distractions and may need to take regular education tests in the emotional or learning support classroom, where there are fewer distractions. Like any other student, she may receive assistance in understanding a question if she respectfully asks for help with such.

11. Brandi may need additional time to complete homework assignments on days when she has sessions with her therapist. Parents, not Brandi, will communicate when this is necessary.

12. Special education teachers, wraparound personnel, the guidance counselor, the one-to-one aide, and when possible regular education teachers need to meet with parents monthly to discuss Brandi's progress and appropriate strategies to assist her in the school environment.
13. Brandi needs individual transportation to and from school.
14. Supervision during free time with peers is critical. Brandi still has not internalized the attachment she is developing with her family, especially with her mother. While well-adjusted children "carry around" their parents' love and acceptance, plus the conscience they have developed, Brandi is just now going through the early stages of this development.
15. Adults should not take Brandi's behavior personally. They should see these acts as expressions of Brandi's frustration with herself and her difficulty controlling her behaviors.

LEAST RESTRICTIVE ENVIRONMENT

If a child with a physical disability—say, a broken arm—is not able to participate in regular school programs, we make accommodations for the child: He or she has an alternative form of gym class and isn't expected to have perfect penmanship with a cast. But how do school districts react to a child with an emotional disturbance like an attachment disorder? By law they must make accommodations and provide educational services with an appropriate IEP.

Schools are not mental health facilities, and school personnel (except those particularly trained) are not therapists. But this being said, it is legally and morally right to support emotional stability and healing in the children in the care of school personnel. Educating themselves is a huge first step for school personnel.

There are different levels of intervention based on the child's disability. Many children can cope with a regular school schedule if they have access to an emotional support classroom or an emotional support aide or counselor. But treating a child with attachment problems like a "normal" student is like offering food to a child who can't open his mouth; it's frustrating for all concerned and won't work. Providing such students with support staff means that they can improve their behavior while remaining in a classroom—the least restrictive environment.

GETTING YOUR CHILD EVALUATED
FOR SPECIAL SERVICES

Parents can request that their child be evaluated by the school district. The district has a specific number of days to complete an evaluation after a written request is made.

Each district has its own system and hierarchy for handling such requests, but generally a multidisciplinary team including the school psychologist is assembled to assess if a child is to be identified as having a handicap. The team evaluates the teachers' observations, the counselor's assessment evaluation, and medical and other outside reports and then if appropriate drafts an IEP. You should remember that you are a critical part of this team! You have the right to receive formal written notice of every meeting and also have the right to obtain whatever reports you wish (a report from an outside psychologist, for example).

From the experiences of many, many of the families with whom I work, I must assume that the district will not be working in your child's best interest. The problem seems always to be money. Hiring special aides or resource-room staff costs money, and the district all too often is looking at its own short-term constraints, not the best interest of the child. I've heard many times the narrow-minded lament, "If we do this for your child, we'll have to do it for all the children." My question is, why *aren't* you doing it for all the children? Placing these children in a regular classroom, without special resources, may save money in the short term; but if their condition deteriorates, the district will have to provide for far more expensive interventions. It's penny-wise and pound-foolish.

After the evaluation report has been prepared (usually ten days after), the group reconvenes to develop the IEP. The district may try to eliminate this ten-day period, saying that if the parents agree and sign the waiver, the IEP can be written right away. Wouldn't that seem like a good thing? I tell parents: in most cases it's best to not sign the IEP right away. The district may well be trying convince you to sign the agreement to accept their first suggestion about meeting your child's needs. Bear in mind that you are dealing with an institution here; they have to consider their limits. Take your time to review the IEP carefully, and don't forget that you are entitled to obtain a second opinion.

Parents should be aware of the applicable laws in their state that deal with the rights of children with special needs. You may need to bring pressure to bear on school districts to follow the law. Many districts do not consider your child's needs to be a priority, and in this situation parents learn that "the squeaky wheel gets the grease."

504 ACCOMMODATIONS

504 accommodations are the accommodations that school districts must legally make for children with medical needs. Here is a 504 accommodations list that I helped to prepared for Mike, the boy from Romania with reactive attachment disorder:

Accommodations:

- Mike should visit the resource room every day, or as needed after initial transition back to school, for help with any academic concerns (particularly abstract thinking), focus, and stress.
- Mike's teacher should be chosen based on his need for structure within the classroom as well as during transitional times. The teacher should be able to provide the structure while employing consequences consistently, as well as provide positive reinforcement to help with self-esteem building. Mike's mother would like to be included in discussions regarding which teacher would best suit Mike's needs.
- Mike should have a classroom aide in class to help him maintain focus and help guide him with peer relationships.
- Preferential seating will be needed to accommodate for Mike's hearing loss in his right ear, his need to be in close proximity to the teacher, and his hypervigilance and need to watch others in the room (by the side window, angled toward class and teacher).
- Mike needs his own "script" for how to act: what is expected of him for things such as changing classes, completing assignments, and interactions with peers in the classroom and at recess.

- Teacher and guidance counselor should coach Mike during the school day as to meeting the requirements of the script. Parents and psychologist will coach him at home and during therapy sessions. The school will provide consequences when Mike does not follow the script.
- Small-group testing is requested to help with focus.
- Mike needs to have the ability to dictate stories and essays into a tape recorder and then write them down, since he has difficulty getting ideas down on paper.
- A homework book needs to be filled out in ink and signed daily by teacher and parents. Consequences need to be given whenever the homework book is left at home or school.
- Consequences for poorly completed or incomplete assignments or behavioral problems need to occur within the school setting. They should be immediate and nonnegotiable, such as completion of work in the school office during recess. The family needs to be removed from exacting consequences for the school, as to do so will affect the therapeutic process of attachment within the home.
- Positive reinforcement (emotional funneling) of appropriate behavior and completion of tasks should be constantly reinforced, both at home and school. An example: "Mom will be so proud of your work!" or "I'll write Mom a note in the homework book to let her know how well you are attending in class!" Emphasis should be put on parental attachment.
- When negative behaviors occur, consequences should be given without lecturing, as this does not affect behavior other than to diminish self-esteem. Mike learns more through the consequence than words; this is typical of children with reactive attachment disorder. Positive reinforcement and consequences must be consistent, following the expectations presented to Mike in order to prevent miscommunication between Mike, the school, and Mike's parents. Mike may attempt to mislead and manipulate the teacher should all expectations and consequences not be consistent. Should there be questions as to how to proceed in regard to a behavior, it is the teacher's responsibility to inform Mike's mother. Together, they will determine how to proceed.

- A secret signal will be designated between teacher and Mike to help Mike recognize when he is off-task and needs to refocus. A private note may be placed on his desk too.
- The guidance counselor will work regularly with Mike on social skills and peer relations. Mike will be included in a social skills group to provide him with supervised opportunities to practice the skills being taught through his therapy and the school counselor.

Concerns That Need to Be Addressed:

- What are the consequences for Mike for behaviors that are not cooperative? Who will enforce them? (The school should be responsible for carrying out the consequences.)
- How can we help Mike with in-class support for transition time between subjects and classes?
- What can be done to help Mike with peer relationship problems during recess? If there are issues, how would they be handled, and by whom? Do recess aides need to be made aware of Mike's needs?
- Can a meeting be arranged just before school starts, or right after, between Mike's teacher, resource room teacher, guidance counselor, and mother to answer any questions about reintegrating Mike back into school? Mike should be included at the end of the meeting so that expectations can be reinforced and he can see that good communication exists between all team members.
- A limited amount of e-mail (specific questions or copies of e-mail to parents) may be sent to Mike's therapist for comment or review.

LETTERS TO TEACHERS

Therapeutic foster parent Gary Flanders has prepared a series of "letters" that parents can send to various persons in their child's life explaining what attachment disorder is and how they can help. Here is his wife's letter to teachers:

Dear Teacher,

My husband and I adopted Liz when she was a toddler. It was the happiest day of our lives. At two-and-a-half she had the biggest, brightest eyes we had ever seen. We planned for her arrival as if she were a birth child. You could not have found a more proud mom and dad on the face of the Earth. We were determined to accept this child into our hearts and lives, and nothing could stop us.

As the days turned into months and the months into seven years, something happened to that happy family. We finally came to the anxious conclusion that we were responsible for what happened in the past seven years, but we were not responsible for what happened in those first two-and-a-half years.

Liz went from lukewarm to cold to violently hating me. I was heartbroken that the little girl who was hesitant to cuddle with me at two-and-a-half was now attacking me every time I came within striking distance. My world was shattered. Not only was my love rejected by my child, I was trapped inside my home with this angry little girl because I could not take her in public without violent tantrums, which oftentimes resulted in me being physically bruised as well as embarrassed. Out of desperation, and after exhausting all resources, I sought help for myself and my child.

After searching for professional help, I discovered that Liz's first two years of life were similar to those of a number of other children in her country. Liz was moved around as an infant and spent months in substitute care. She was with her birth mother only very briefly before being taken by a number of relatives. I cannot explain to you how I felt when I finally saw the social service record and discovered what had happened to my precious daughter. But even worse was how I felt when I found out that our love was not enough to overcome what had happened. I gave her my heart and that was not enough.

The disease I alluded to is called attachment disorder. It means that for whatever reason, she never emotionally bonded to anyone. Please don't be skeptical and think that we have sold out to pop psychology. We are loving parents and would never buy into the latest mumbo-jumbo to explain away problems we are having with our child. This is the scariest, most emotionally wrenching thing we have ever had to face. Please don't think we are horrible parents or bad people.

We need your understanding and help in providing a safe place for our child, your student, to become a loving, caring human being.

After spending untold money and time searching for someone to understand what we were going through, we came across some parents and therapists who deal specifically with this disorder. We had gone through every form of therapy there is, and Liz only seemed to get worse. We had read every parenting book available and attended too many boring parenting seminars, all of which dealt with something other than what our daughter was acting out at home. Until we found someone who knew our daughter and what she had gone through, we were becoming angry, bitter people.

We have learned that children with this type of problem respond best to a tight, loving atmosphere. For some reason, probably a physiological genesis that has to do with how the brain is actually damaged when a child is severely neglected and abused, children with attachment disorder fear being the one in charge. But this thing they fear, they fight extremely hard to always have. It makes for a frustrated child until they are with someone who loves that child enough to take charge of him or her. A no-nonsense approach to Liz allows her to relax, no longer being hypervigilant and planning on how to control others by acting out. She can, in a sense, be a child again, not a neglect/abuse survivor. We love our daughter enough to let her know that she no longer has to be a controlling tyrant, but she can go back to being something that was interrupted long ago—a child.

Simple things go a long way in having an adult/child relationship with children with attachment difficulties. An old-fashioned thing like having your "yes mean yes" and "no mean no" actually makes Liz feel safe. If she feels that she can whine or plead and still get her way, she is back in charge and not feeling safe. When she does not feel safe she acts out, testing you and giving you another opportunity to establish who is in charge.

We also found that Liz was not internalizing our love or even allowing it to enter her world because she fears intimacy so much. It is not hard to understand that for someone abandoned so early in life, love is a painful emotion with no joy involved. Liz can actually do much better with strangers or someone she can get away from easily. The closeness of a family feels very dangerous to her. This is where parents who are attempting to love these children come across looking like harsh people to those who are unaware. The thought is that surely there must be something wrong with mom or the family because this child does not act all that out of the ordinary in my classroom but is being described as a monster at home. Please don't think poorly of me for giving this wonderfully difficult child a chance to live a happy, loving life. I love her enough to parent in a way that seems tough right now, so I can teach her that love can be joyful.

My hope for you is that you will understand, even a little, why my relationship with my child is not what you would categorize as ordinary. She has such wonderful potential, and she had such a sad early life. She resists my love so adamantly, and she desperately needs a strong mom. She presents such unusual behavior because she has such a damaged spirit. She needs strong people in her life because she is the most cunning person I have ever seen.

Please feel free to ask me more about this wonderfully scary little girl with the brightest eyes in the world. I love her more than ever and am determined to give her the best chances in life and to help her regain the hope she lost so long ago.

ABOUT HEATHER

Heather was adopted at age one from a Russian orphanage. She joined her adoptive parents and a previously adopted girl from Russia. She underwent six months of intensive attachment therapy, with a highly successful outcome. Her adoptive mother wrote the following about her daughter.

> I took Heather to her first gymnastics class this afternoon, praying for the past week that she would enjoy herself and be compliant for the teacher. Well, you wouldn't believe how well she did. The tears running down my cheeks as I laughed were tears of joy. I am sure the other parents thought I was a kooky mother. I have to say that that was one of the happiest moments that I have had in the past two years! She just fit in so well, and with her being the youngest in the class she held her own and just had a great time. She was so happy after the class and hasn't stopped talking about it since. Needless to say, I am so proud of her.

10

THERAPY: HOW TO GET PROFESSIONAL HELP FOR CHILDREN WITH RAD

There is such a difference between the way I thought before and the way I think now. Before I started therapy I thought of my parents as the enemy, or like guards at a prison, that I had to outwit or escape. Now I see us as a team working together.

—JADE

Therapeutic approaches must appreciate the persistent fear state that traumatized children experience and must be directed at the areas of the brain which mediate this alarm-fear-terror continuum.

—BRUCE PERRY, M.D.

If your child's attachment issues are affecting his quality of life, you may want to seek help from a professional therapist. This is a chapter about how we psychotherapeutically treat attachment disorders. It is all about creating a safe place inside your little one's body and brain and teaching internal self-regulation, because safety and self-regulation are critical to learning and to leading a healthy, happy life.

FINDING HELP

I am convinced that many times the reason parents refuse to accept that their child has a problem of any definable magnitude is that they are not sure they can make a positive difference. But if parents are given tools to help their child, then maybe they can accept the challenge to make a difference.

If you have concerns about whether your child is "normal" or whether an attachment problem exists, remember that *you* are the most important person in your child's life. Act on your suspicions. I often hear from parents who wish they had brought their children in for evaluation earlier. From a treatment standpoint, the younger a child begins treatment for attachment problems, the higher the chances of successful attachment.

Look for a mental health professional who is willing to listen to your questions and concerns and who will acknowledge that you know your child better than anyone else. Lay out everything that is troubling you about the child and even your own feelings about what you're experiencing. Does this sound as if I'm trying to drum up business? I'm not; believe me, all truly caring mental health practitioners would rather be put out of business than see the heartaches we do every day.

Finding a therapist who understands trauma is critical. The American Psychiatric Association gives this advice to parents seeking help for RAD:

- Seek a comprehensive evaluation by an appropriately trained, qualified, and experienced mental health professional prior to the initiation of any treatment plan.
- Ask questions about the results of the evaluation.
- Make sure you understand in detail the risks as well as the potential benefits of any intervention.
- Feel free to seek a second opinion if you have questions or concerns.

The responsibilities of an attachment therapist, as set forth by ATTACh, are as follows:

- To promote, develop, and enhance a reciprocal attachment to the primary caregiver of the child
- To be well trained in attachment and bonding treatment method options
- To continue to develop skills through education specific to attachment
- To use supervision and professional consultation for personal support
- To support the authority and values of the parents
- To provide skills development for parents of the hurt child
- To take an active and directive stance in working with the child and family on core issues that they may find difficult to address (ATTACh, 2003)

While seeking a therapist, remember that treatment for attachment disorder does not occur only in the therapist's office. Above all, these children need stability and consistency, as the foundation on which your attachment work can be built. Your child's sense of trust in the world is so tenuous that if you're not working on attachment issues twenty-four hours a day, seven days a week, that slender thread of trust is apt to break completely. Be prepared to follow up vigorously at home what is learned in the therapist's office.

DIAGNOSIS

Children who exhibit signs of RAD need a comprehensive psychiatric assessment. Particular care must be taken to distinguish RAD from one of the Pervasive Developmental Disorders, such as Autistic Disorder.

—AMERICAN PSYCHIATRIC ASSOCIATION, 2002 POSITION
STATEMENT ON REACTIVE ATTACHMENT DISORDER

Because RAD is not yet widely known, getting the correct diagnosis is critical for you and your child. Many children with RAD are misdiagnosed as having attention deficit hyperactivity disorder (ADHD), oppositional defiant disorder, or a disorder on the autism spectrum. While in many ways behaviors of various disorders look similar, the treatments for these disorders can differ greatly from those effective for RAD.

Many parents have told me that medical professionals have given their child numerous diagnoses, but no treatment seemed to work. Do you remember Mike, the boy adopted from Romania, in chapter 4? His parents had taken him to numerous therapists starting at age three, and he was treated for attention deficit disorder, with no effect. When his mother finally read about RAD on the Internet, "it all fell into place. 'This is him!' I thought."

"I wish we had had more information at the beginning, but I'm not sure it was out there," she said. "We anticipated problems, but nothing like this. . . . We spent years and years trying to figure out what's wrong with my son. Lucky for me I have some background in mental health. I don't know how a family without that knowledge could possibly manage it."

One assessment tool that is very effective in helping to thoroughly diagnose problems is the Trauma Symptom Checklist for Children (TSCC; Briere 1996). In this test, the child rates, on a scale of 0 to 3, how often each of a list of thoughts, feelings, and behaviors occurs. The list includes six categories of questions:

- Anxiety (generalized anxiety, worry, specific fears)
- Depression (unhappiness, loneliness, suicidal thoughts)
- Anger (angry thoughts, feelings, and behaviors, hatred, arguing and fighting)
- Post-traumatic stress (intrusive thoughts, sensations and memories of painful events, nightmares)
- Dissociation (derealization, mind going blank, emotional numbing, pretending to be someone or somewhere else, memory problems)
- Sexual concerns (two subscales: sexual preoccupation and sexual distress)

If you seek professional help, ask your therapist to administer this test. The full fifty-four-item test takes about twenty minutes to complete, and it can be scored in about ten minutes. (A forty-four-question version omitting sexual concerns takes slightly less time to complete and score.) Getting the right diagnosis early on may save you years of frustration and ineffectual treatment.

PREPARING CHILDREN FOR THERAPY

I wish so much I could change my past and erase all the errors I made, but RAD is like insanity. The more insane you are, the less you believe it. I thought so differently. I was so delusional back then that I can't even put myself in that place anymore. Thankfully! I was given up as a hopeless case by one therapist. Now I can understand why she thought that. I am just so thankful my parents didn't give up on me, but kept searching for help. They had faith God would send the right help, and He did.

—JADE

Evaluating and treating children with complex child psychiatric conditions such as Reactive Attachment Disorder is challenging. There are no simple solutions or magic answers. However, close and ongoing collaboration between the child's family and the treatment team will increase the likelihood of a successful outcome.

—AMERICAN PSYCHIATRIC ASSOCIATION, 2002 POSITION
STATEMENT ON REACTIVE ATTACHMENT DISORDER

Once you have found a therapist and received a diagnosis of RAD, treatment can begin. Here is how I ask parents to understand the incredible risk we are asking their child to take in therapy: Pretend you are standing on the edge of a high cliff. Standing next to you is someone you know only on the surface. You may have known him or her for a long period of time, but you have little or only superficial emotional intimacy with him or her.

Now pretend that this person says to you, "Hold my hand and jump off the cliff with me. Trust me; it will be okay. I'll make sure you land safely and won't be hurt." Add to this picture the fact that someone has asked you to do this before: this is not the first time you've been asked to take this leap. Finally, imagine that this person is saying to you that he or she will keep you from hurting yourself if you jump with him or her. But you *know* that you'll be killed.

Why would you ever, in your right mind, take such a chance? Can you imagine yourself doing something so foolish? Deep down, these children know something's not right with their situation. But given their background, what we ask them to do in therapy—to give up an element of control—is more frightening to them than remaining in their current state. "Giving up," as in giving up control, is truly a life-and-death matter to them because their early patterning equates being in control with surviving.

Adults who realize that they have a phobia or some other mental health problem have a motivation to change. But these children do not have such a motivation because they don't realize that there is another, healthier way of behaving. In addition, the indications that they operate at higher levels of chemical functioning helps explain our experience that they are highly resistant to therapy. Sensitivity to their fears and patience with their resistance will help them ultimately accept the help that is being offered them.

THE THERAPY ENVIRONMENT

A good clinic will take pains to make sure that every part of the environment is a therapeutic one. Some clinics avoid the use of volatile chemicals in the carpet, furniture, and paint, chemicals that can stress the already sensitive nervous systems of the clients. Walls should not be bright and "cheerful," like you might find in other pediatric facilities. Colors should be calm and soothing, the lighting natural, not fluorescent. You should try to replicate this therapeutic environment at home as well. It's all part of the 24/7 nature of dealing with attachment issues.

THE TREATMENT PROCESS

Research on treatment for RAD is in its infancy. As Calhoun and Resnick (1993) state, "Very little controlled treatment research has been conducted with victims of . . . civilian traumas. However, a wide variety of approaches have been described anecdotally or in uncontrolled case reports. These include psychodynamic psychotherapy, biofeedback, flooding, systematic desensitization, cognitive therapy, and approaches aimed at specific [behavioral] problems."

There is much controversy surrounding treatment of children who have sustained traumatic childhood experiences. The therapies discussed in the next few sections are those we have found to be most effective given our current state of information and experience. Always, *always*, a child's safety comes first.

Synergistic Trauma and Attachment Therapy

The treatment for RAD that is offered at our clinic is called Synergistic Trauma and Attachment Therapy. This treatment approach seeks to enhance parental attachment by first and foremost promoting trust. The goals are as follows:

- Teaching and modeling for the family the experiences of providing a predictable, nurturing, and supportive environment; raising a child with RAD requires learning parenting skills that are often counterintuitive to the ways we raise children without RAD
- Reforming the child's inner working model (what he or she believes about him or herself) from negative to positive
- Reducing the levels of hypervigilance and hyperactivity ingrained in the child's brain
- Educating, supporting, and nurturing the family in order to best nurture the child
- Treating the child at his or her emotional, not chronological, age
- Working with other professionals in the child's life to make sure everyone is, as much as possible, working in concert with each other

A cornerstone of this treatment is the recognition of the dynamic nature of children, RAD, and consequently therapy plans. The child and the disorder are both dynamic and ever-changing, so therapy must be too. The therapist must constantly reassess where the child and family are and how they are changing (sometimes even within a session), tailoring treatment appropriately and carefully interweaving any technique that will help. Therapists using this system can sometimes run into trouble with health insurance companies, who insist on receiving well laid-out treatment plans for patients before they will authorize treatment. But a static treatment plan will not be effective to the changing needs of the child, and there is not yet a complete and set "clinical pathway" for RAD therapy.

How long does this process take? One noted professional in the field has suggested that for every six months the child has experienced untreated attachment disorder, it takes one month of intensive therapy to reverse. Treatment is likely to be lengthy. However, when I explain that we cannot give a predictable timeline, but will work as quickly as we can within the bounds of safe treatment, most parents say to me, "We'll do whatever it takes."

Alleviating Cognitive Dissonance

One cornerstone of successful therapy is the alleviation of what therapists call cognitive dissonance. A major goal of therapy is to boost the self-concept and morale of the children. But because of their early experiences of rejection, these children don't think much of themselves. So when you praise your child, in the child's eyes, frankly, you don't know what you're talking about—there's a "dissonance," a discrepancy between what the child hears you say and what he believes about himself. General praise, no matter how well intentioned, paradoxically only adds to the child's distrust of you and the world.

How do we battle this deep-seated feeling? In therapy, the key is to focus on praise that is specific and concrete—praise that is in some sense irrefutable and thus *not* dissonant. A therapist must search for an activity or skill that the children already has—and *knows* he has. This might be walking down the hall well or being a great yeller, jumper, or scrambler—anything that the child does well, that she *knows* she does well, and that can be complimented.

Once the therapist finds such an activity, specific praise should follow, funneled, as always, to the parents: "Mom must be very proud of you." Go over the top with it—anything to help the child get over that shame and mistrust at the core of his self-concept.

Systematic Desensitization

One of the first things I remember about therapy was the skin/eye contact Mom and I practiced during sessions. Another change was Lark said no social activity for a while, giving my mom and me a chance to bond. This was one of the hardest things I had to deal with in therapy. When I came to Lark I was still enmeshed in my problems such as lying, stealing, manipulating, etc., but as months passed we saw improvement.

—JADE

Another important element of therapy is a process called *systematic desensitization*, which involves developing a "culture of safety." RAD children often feel threatened by normal stimuli and everyday activities, often activities involving touch, such as sitting on a parent's lap or even sitting next to or being touched by a parent. Systematic desensitization is designed to help the child relax and participate in these normal activities without responding with a "fight, flight, or freeze" reaction. "Desensitization" has the connotation of taking something away, and that is true: as therapists we want the child to become less sensitive to normal stimuli or give up unusually strange or unhealthy hyperreactions to otherwise healthy stimuli. However, we also want to add something: a feeling that the child is safe while in Mom's lap or arms, and eventually in the world.

Systematic desensitization starts with something as basic as being touched by Mom for thirty seconds—a simple act that can terrify many children with RAD. To begin, for example, we ask the child to sit on Mom's lap for a short time, to do just a little bit of this "scary work," and then quickly return the child back to a place of safety, away from the touch he instinctively fears. Once he is back in his safety zone, we follow up with deep breathing and "floppy doll" exercises to help him relax. Once the child has experienced the activity and seen that he is quickly returned to safety and a feeling of calm, we gradually stretch the amount of time spent in the "danger zone" and give the child the repeated experience of being returned to safety over and over gain. With time and experience, the child will begin to realize, "It's okay for me to relax in Mom's lap because I know she won't hurt me. I'm safe here with her."

Desensitization engages the child's protective mechanism, but it should also be fun. We use games that involve touching and I encourage parents to touch their children deliberately (while making it appear accidental!), sometimes even counting the number of times that contact is made ("Look! I touched your cheek again! That's three today!"). Kids love this kind of counting. The point is to make the child aware that touch is safe, fun, and even soothing and comforting, but without forcing it to further imbed emotional trauma.

Therapists can reinforce the safety of touch by touching the children frequently. In professional circles, touch between a therapist and a patient has long been considered inappropriate. But for children with attachment issues, touch is a vital component of therapy. A recent article in the *Journal of Neurophysiology* shows that key parts of the brain involved in attachment behaviors have been found to respond to "neutral tactile stimulation"—in other words, touch (Hagen et al. 2002).

Practicing eye contact is important as well. Most children with RAD have perfected the ability to pretend to look at people, but not really make the eyeball-to-eyeball, soul-to-soul connection. Playing games like peekaboo can help show children that making true eye contact is not scary.

With repeated exposure and lengthening of time spent in the "danger zone," the child's body learns to react in a healthy rather than hyperreactive manner to normal stimuli. If the child is old enough, he will begin to realize that his brain is in charge of what his body does.

EEG Biofeedback, or Neurofeedback

Around February I started additional therapy called neurofeedback. When I began I was a terribly uncoordinated runner and couldn't handle large crowds without getting exhausted and stressed out. I couldn't even really relax, hypervigilance being a part of the disorder. Now I am fine in large crowds and can run moderately fast— I even enjoy it! NFB also helped me to just plain old relax.

*—*JADE

Another increasingly common type of therapy for RAD is a computerized technique called EEG (electroencephalograph) biofeedback, also known as neurofeedback or brainwave biofeedback. For children with RAD, the goal is to help the children regulate their own brain activity and learn to calm the areas in their brain that are overreacting. As we learned in earlier chapters, RAD is a neurological problem, so brain function must be addressed if the child's behavior is to change. Luckily, the human brain is amazingly adaptable and capable of learning to improve its own performance. This painless and noninvasive technique shows great promise in training the brain to improve its own function.

EEG biofeedback is, in the simplest of terms, exercise for the brain. By monitoring the EEG, we can show the children their own brain's rhythm on a computer screen and teach them to strengthen the rhythms of calmness and relaxation and thus facilitate the formation of a therapeutic bond with their parents.

Extensive testing and analysis can precede the first EEG biofeedback session, sometimes including computer-assisted assessment tools. A commonly used tool is the TOVA (test of variables of attention). In this twenty-minute test, the child sits in front of a computer screen, and one of two patterns is flashed on the screen in a random sequence (or, in the auditory version, the child hears a high-pitched or a low-pitched sound in a random sequence). Unlike the EEG biofeedback training itself, with the TOVA the child is instructed to click a button when the target pattern (or sound) appears and *not* to click it when the other one (the nontarget) appears. Clicking appropriately (at the target pattern) is a measure of attention. Clicking inappropriately (at the nontarget pattern) is a measure of impulsivity because the child must hold back from clicking. The computer also measures the speed and consistency of the child's responses to provide further information about neurological function.

The TOVA is an objective, standardized test used to assess an individual's attention abilities and performance. The test is not language based and is culturally sensitive. Although it was developed for use with attention deficit hyperactivity disorder, it can help screen for disorders of attention, impulsivity, and other neurologic functions in any child. It can also be used to measure medication responses and monitor treatment over time. The TOVA can be repeated because there is no "learning" from earlier testing; thus, after a course of treatment, repeating the test can measure the child's improvement. (For more information about the TOVA assessment tool, visit www.tova.net.)

After a child is tested to establish baselines for attention and impulsivity, the actual EEG biofeedback session may begin. During the session, the child sits in a comfortable chair, often in the parent's lap. He faces a computer monitor, and sensors are placed on the child's head with a conductive paste (the paste is easily removed). The location of the sensors is based on what areas of the brain would benefit from calming. No electricity is put into the brain; the sensors are there only to monitor the brain waves. It's a one-way fiberoptic path from the child's brain to the computer. The child learns how to regulate brain functioning by what happens in the game on the computer screen.

The child simply plays a specially adapted computer game like Pac-Man, using only his brain waves to do so: no joystick or controller! The paradox is that it doesn't work if the child tries by thinking hard; in fact, the harder he tries, the worse he will do because it is the brain waves that produce the calm, alert state that make the game work, not the high-frequency waves normally used for solving problems. These high-frequency waves can be the ones related to anxiety, hypervigilance, and hyperreactivity. When the brain produces inappropriate brain waves, the game will slow down and the Pac-Man will lose his appetite. When the child produces the calming, self-regulating brain waves that we want to encourage, the game speeds up and the Pac-Man readily devours his opponents. Very low-frequency waves may also be inappropriate and can be discouraged by the game's settings.

In the computer game, the brain is rewarded for moving in the direction of better control and a calm, alert state. The rewards are the sights, sounds, and points scored in the game. Repetition leads to gradual learning of better function. Children learn to relax and enjoy sitting in Mom's lap in a calm state within the framework of a nurturing environment.

Bob Patterson, director of the the Neuro Enhancement Center and a licensed physical therapist and biofeedback specialist, has used neurofeedback for years. For each patient, Bob and the parents target about six behaviors that they want to monitor—for instance, opposition, aggressive behavior, compulsive behavior, tantrums, nightmares, and eye contact. The parents fill out a questionnaire before each session, rating the child's progress in each of the behaviors since the last session, using a 0 to 4 rating scale. Bob charts these to keep track of each child's progress. He also keeps track of the data from each EEG biofeedback session on computer disks and coordinates closely with the other therapists working with the child to monitor and modify the feedback. Neurofeedback should be only one component of a comprehensive therapy plan. But it has shown great promise in disorders such as RAD, attention deficit hyperactivity, epilepsy, depression, anxiety, addictions, chronic pain, stroke, traumatic brain injury, autoimmune dysfunction, and sleep disorders. Even athletes, performing artists, and executives are using it to enhance their performance, concentration, and awareness. There are no known adverse side effects to EEG biofeedback, provided that the training is conducted under professional guidance.

For more information about EEG biofeedback, see Robbins (1996, 2000), Hill and Castro (2002), and the websites www.eegspectrum.com and brianothmerfoundation.org.

EMDR

EMDR has been very helpful for our son. He handles feelings of anxiety so much better. When he is anxious about something, he usually doesn't stay that way twenty-four hours a day. He can engage in other activities and have fun.

—PARENTS OF A NINE-YEAR-OLD BOY
ADOPTED FROM RUSSIA AT AGE FIVE

EMDR (eye movement desensitization and reprocessing) is another innovative treatment that has become popular in recent years. Developed in 1987 by psychologist Francine Shapiro, it has been used to help trauma survivors as well as patients with depression, addictions, and phobias. Using rhythmic bilateral stimulation, including eye movements, the treatment is another way of activating the brain's information processing system.

The goals of EMDR as an intervention are as follows:

1. To focus attention on a specific memory, thought, image, or emotion
2. To unravel strings of disturbing traumatic experience, possibly providing missing detail or data towards resolution
3. To eliminate irrational components of fears to allow other expressed or hidden affect to be processed
4. To reinforce more adaptive behaviors
5. To build positive, realistic beliefs
6. To strengthen ego and instill inner resources to build self-esteem

In EMDR therapy, the parents and child usually have an initial consultation with the therapist. During this consultation and subsequent sessions, the therapist will take a detailed history of the patient, learn about his or her family background, develop rapport and trust with the patient and family, and give them the opportunity to ask questions about EMDR and about her own qualifications.

During this initial meeting, the therapist is likely also to take steps to determine the child's developmental age in order to devise the best treatment plan for the child's stage of development. She will try to establish the challenges the child is facing, perhaps asking the child to draw a picture of what is bothering him or her and a picture of a safe or happy place. (Older children can do this verbally.) They discuss what is frightening the child, how much it is bothering him, and where in the body that worry is manifested.

After the initial consultation, the therapist develops a treatment plan specifically for that child and always with the client's needs and desires first in her mind. During the next several meetings, they will begin establishing a rapport and working towards developing an EMDR protocol. EMDR uses the concept of alternating stimulation to the right and left sides of the brain to achieve its effect, but the exact nature of the treatment can vary from therapist to therapist. In our clinic, the therapist does not use eye movement but rather audio tones and vibrations to create this alternating stimulation. The child wears headphones and listens to tones that alternate from ear to ear. The therapist controls the speed, volume, and intensity of the tones. The child also holds a small oval device in each hand that vibrates simultaneously with the sounds.

The alternating stimuli can help a traumatized child "process" his or her experience of trauma differently than he has in the past. Often traumatized children become "stuck" in an emotional phase and don't understand why. When trauma is experienced, it often becomes locked in the right (emotional) side of the brain. By stimulating both the right (emotional) and the left (rational) side of the brain simultaneously, therapists are noting that this pattern can be broken.

In our clinic, before the patient listens to the sounds and feels the vibrations, the therapist encourages the patient to focus on the negative image and the feelings that accompany this image, to feel where this manifests in the body. She then instructs the client to tell her when anything changes from the original image or to notice any changes in the body. The bilateral stimulation is applied. She often has to prompt her young clients because they are often not very good at "reading" their own bodies and noticing changes. As the child experiences a cognitive or somatic (body) change, the therapist stops the bilateral stimulation and the child reports the change to the therapist.

She also uses scales (say, 1 to 10) at the beginning and end of sessions to assess how much the feeling of trauma has reduced in its impact and to gauge how the worry has decreased. She finds that after the uppermost worry has been handled, other concerns or traumas arise, some of which the child was initially unaware of. She treats this with additional EMDR sessions or other appropriate therapies offered at the clinic. Once a particular issue is no longer bothersome, a positive installation is completed, using the same method.

The effects of EMDR will last beyond the actual session as the brain is still processing the stimuli, so the child may be irritable or have bad dreams. It's important for parents to keep in touch with the therapist between sessions. They may also want to create a "safe place" for their child at home to allow the child to retreat, relax, and feel secure—a favorite chair in the living room, a seat by the window where she can watch the birds or squirrels outside, a "circle of safety" space in the playroom that no one else can enter or "mess up." The only things in the child's safe place should be items he can use to comfort him (stuffed animal, favorite blanket)—ones which cannot hurt him in any way and which you won't mind if are ruined. The safe place should be within your line of vision or hearing. Your child needs to know that he is safe there, and this means he needs to know you will see if there's a problem and will respond immediately.

Theraplay

Theraplay is a therapeutic technique developed by the Theraplay Institute. The following information is based on material from Phyllis Booth, director of training at the Theraplay Institute.

Theraplay is based on two principles: attuned responsiveness to the child's signals, feelings, and needs, and engaging in mutually enjoyable social interactions within the context of an intimate and continuous relationship. Parents must remember that adopted children are likely to be emotionally much younger than their chronological age: an eight-year-old child may have the emotional needs of a three-year-old or even a toddler. Parents should make allowances for this and not expect a child always to "act your age." On the positive side, he or she may respond well to these childlike games and activities.

Theraplay has four dimensions: structure, engagement, nurture, and challenge:

1. Providing *structure* in a child's life, including during play, makes him or her feel secure. With an adopted child, you may need to provide a highly structured environment with plenty of supervision. Remember that an older child may need a level of supervision and assistance more suited to a much younger child. Ask yourself, "What would a toddler need in this situation?"
2. *Engagement* means being attuned to a child's feelings (stimulated or calm), helping him or her to become aware of those feelings and the feelings of others. This is the basis for self-regulation, and for empathy. When playing, parents should make sure their children do not become overly stimulated. Try a slower, calming game after, say, a more rambunctious, physically active one.
3. *Nurture* conveys the message that you love the child and will take care of him or her. This can be difficult with a child who is

determined not to let you take care of him. It can be a challenge to find a substitute for cuddling and holding with such a child. Try feeding him a special food (perhaps a Popsicle in the summer heat), something he will especially like, while holding him close. Make a game of rubbing lotion on her arms while having her try to get away (you can fall over in mock surprise as she escapes!).

4. *Challenge* also must be suitable for the child's emotional age. The goal is to encourage your child to move ahead and to become confident and competent. You wouldn't expect a toddler to make his bed by himself, so don't expect your seven-year-old adopted child to do so. Instead, let him hide under the covers as you try to smooth the sheets, baffled at the lump you keep finding there. You and he both will be amused when you pretend to realize that it is actually your son! Together you can then smooth the bedclothes.

Booth (2002) summarizes Theraplay's benefits in attachment therapy as follows: "The goal of all your interactions with your child is to help her learn how to share fun and love. Your child can learn to accept structure and adult direction in the context of playful games. She can learn to engage with you in joyful play. She can begin to know the comfort of being taken care of as you help her accept your nurturing care. She can experience herself as competent and successful as she comes to enjoy your challenging games."

Theraplay focuses on simple one-on-one interactions instead of on toys, trips, and special outings. Parents learn to schedule one-on-one time with Mommy or Daddy each and every day, no matter how busy the family gets. Finnell (1996) describes Theraplay this way:

Theraplay is especially useful in the early stages of adoption, because it allows parents to "check out" the child, get to know her preferences, and learn what she enjoys. The Theraplay model teaches us that these activities should be provided for the child, without the child needing to demand them. Many successful adoptions have resulted when parents go about forming an attachment in much the same way that biological parents do with their infants. This means accepting, even enjoying, regressive behavior, and finding out "what will work" with this child. Theraplay, again, is helpful to coax the child into doing things "our way" because the child's individual needs are recognized, her individuality celebrated.

Adoptive parents do well if they practice the three R's, P's, and C's to develop attachment:

- Rules, Routines, and Rituals
- Patience, Persistence, and Play
- Contact, Conversation, and Cuddling

Adoptive children need lots of attentive responsiveness and enthusiasm about them. Holding and cuddling are critical; playful give and take must occur. Baby games are fine to meet regressive needs. Enough structure and limits must be present, and personalized attention such as that given in Theraplay is a foundation to begin the attachment process. More information about Theraplay can be found at www.theraplay.org.

Reparenting

Reparenting, pioneered by Daniel Hughes, is a parenting or therapeutic treatment in which parents help to bring the child back to a point at which he or she feels safe; they build from there onto each progressive developmental stage. The parents return their child to a place where it is comfortable for him to relax and let nature take its developmental course. This therapy helps children who are "stuck" in some phase of development to get beyond the roadblock.

Camp Celebration

Researchers at Texas Christian University (TCU) conducted a fascinating and encouraging experiment in the summer of 1999, offering an opportunity for twenty internationally adopted children to attend three-week sessions at Camp Celebration in Fort Worth, Texas. The goal was to try to reverse attachment disorder by intensive sensory stimulation and a focus on attachment behaviors. One group of campers were four- to eight-year-olds; the other were ten- to fifteen-year-olds.

The program was a joint project with the TCU Psychology Department, the Texas Parents' Network for Post-Institutionalized Children, and the Child Study Center in Fort Worth. The camp was the brainchild of Karyn Purvis, a TCU doctoral student, and Kathie Seidel, chapter president of the Texas Parent's Network for Post-Institutionalized Children.

As a summary of the program states, "Children with attachment disorders display traits such as stealing, lying about the obvious, cruelty, and food hoarding. These become necessary survival skills in places where no one seems to care about them, such as an orphanage, where basic physical needs may be met but not emotional needs. The result is a change in the brain, an actual physical dysfunction."

"A child who has never been connected to anyone lacks moral development because moral development hinges on 'I care about you and don't want to hurt you,'" said Purvis. "Social development follows on 'You are responsive to me; therefore, I want to be responsive to others.'"

The programs involved typical summer-camp activities such as arts and crafts, games, play, and drama. In addition, the campers formulated "social contracts" focusing on behaviors they wanted to work on, such as "I will show respect" and "I will practice accepting 'no.'" The campers and counselors would also "act out" typical daily situations, first modeling the "wrong" behavior and then the correct one. For instance, a counselor would pretend to be a mother asking a camper to make his bed. The skits were videotaped so the children could see how they looked when they were modeling the incorrect behavior.

In addition, the children engaged in "stranger practice" to help them learn from whom it was appropriate to seek affection. "Indiscriminate friendliness is a major problem among post-institutional children," said Purvis.

Sensory activities, thought to help organize brain functions and thinking processes, were also on the camp agenda. Even the types of snacks provided were part of the plan: sweet snacks are calming and sour tastes are alerting. Bubble gum was freely available because chewing gum provides deep muscle pressure.

The results were promising. There was a 31 percent decrease in typical attachment disorder behaviors such as lying, stealing, cruelty, and food hoarding at the end of the session (41 percent in the younger group, 21 percent in the older group). The children showed a 19 percent increase in positive attachment behaviors such as willingness to communicate, increase in eye contact, cooperation with the family, and genuine expressions of physical affection.

According to David Cross, a TCU psychology professor who helped administer the camp, the results in some cases were "really dramatic." In two instances, he said, "the parents completely broke down in tears of joy; the impact on their family was monumental. And they had already started the paperwork to let those kids go."

Purvis said one mother told her that her six-year-old son had asked her to rock him to sleep, "something he had never done in the three years since she brought him home. These children have such trust issues that something so basic as falling asleep in their adoptive parent's arms is a major challenge."

Purvis said that three campers went into "spontaneous regression; that is, they went back to infantile behaviors that they missed or were denied in the orphanages. It appears that what they got at camp allowed them to organize their thinking enough to regress to a time when they needed to bond to someone but couldn't. But this time there was a loving parent at home, and they connected."

Cognitive Behavioral Therapy

Cognitive behavioral therapy (CBT) is a therapy that addresses the cognitive function of emotional dysfunction. Put simply, it involves helping a person become aware of how his behavior affects his emotions and thoughts and conversely how his thoughts and emotions affect his behavior. Perceptions are subjective by their very nature and can be distorted under stress—and children who have attachment issues are *always* under stress.

CBT therapy is rarely the primary treatment method for RAD, but it can be helpful in the later stages of attachment therapy, after the child has formed a strong attachment and he or she is receptive to this type of treatment. For more information about CBT, visit www.cognitive-behavior-therapy.org.

Other Types of Therapy

Depending on the client's particular situation, we can add other modalities to the treatment menu:

- Occupational or physical therapy focusing on issues of sensory integration
- Movement therapies such as integrated awareness, work by Feldenkrais, and Brain Gym, which encourage the brain and body to work together to resolve trauma, improve neurologic function, and promote emotional healing
- Sound therapies
- Music therapy, which can help children learn to self-soothe, become more in tune with their inner selves, and expand their sense of the world in a nonthreatening way

MEDICATIONS

The use of medications with children and adolescents with attachment problems is a tricky one, fraught with concerns on the part of professionals and parents alike. The medications most commonly used with children who exhibit mood disorders have not actually been approved for use with children and are therefore inherently risky to use.

Many children and adolescents, too, are placed on more than one medication to treat their complexities of behaviors and to counteract the negative effects of the first medications they are on. It becomes a guessing game (and *not* a safe one) to try to evaluate the effects of these medications— positive and negative—while the children are becoming victims of the polypharmacological attempts to help parents, schools, and the children themselves. We are not aware of the long-term effects of many of the drugs most commonly used. Even those that have been on the market for many years are surprising us with little-known, -reported, or -studied long-term negative consequences. Sometimes these effects just don't show up for years.

Given these concerns, why are medications so commonly used for RAD? One reason is that parents are desperate to help their children deal with the obvious pain and out-of-control behavior they exhibit.

Another reason is less altruistic: insurance companies, and sometimes physicians themselves, would rather treat the short-term problem than address the underlying, more difficult to treat, cause. It does little good in the long term to treat children without determining the original problem and finding the healthiest cure. We need to stop masking the problem with medications and start doing the extensive, exhaustive, yet critical job of learning what is really happening inside the brains and functioning of these little ones. How else can we truly help them?

One of our initial jobs in working with children who are on medication is to consult with the medical professional early in the assessment period. We must then stay in touch with that medical person, for many reasons. One is that with proper treatment, the medication dosage can often be reduced and still achieve the same results. When a child begins to heal, keeping him or her on the same doses of medicine becomes, by default, *overmedicating* the child. This is an dangerous medical, psychological, and humanitarian insult to the child.

All that being said, sometimes medication is useful, even necessary. We do not always know the biological, genetic background of the children we treat. They may be coming to us with a genetic history of which we are unaware. In this country, birth records in many states are sealed, and adopted children—even adults— cannot have access to what might be life-saving information about their medical genetic codes. These children may have psychiatric or medical conditions that require psychotropic treatment, at least until psychological interventions can help the child control his or her own behavior.

At times, too, medicine helps allow the psychotherapeutic treatment to be effective. For example, if the child's ability to focus is next to zero, it does little good (in fact, in the end it does harm) to try to effect a discussion or therapeutic interaction with the child. Medications may allow the child to focus and thus make progress with psychological therapy.

RESIDENTIAL TREATMENT FACILITIES

Although traditional outpatient therapies work wonders for many children, a minority of children will not respond to them. In these cases, sometimes inpatient treatment is needed to prevent the child from harming himself or others. Unfortunately, because RAD is a newly recognized disorder, few residential treatment facilities (RTFs) have the understanding or commitment to be effective with these children.

The problems with RTFs can be several. First, as noted by the American Psychiatric Association in its position statement on RAD (2002), hospitalization defeats the very goal of therapy: attachment to the parents. Kathy Caruso, Ph.D., an adoptive mother with extensive professional experience in inpatient and partial hospitalization settings, agrees: "These kids get group therapy and learn about anger management [in an RTF], but what they need is to attach."

In fact, children with RAD may seem to flourish at an RTF exactly because they don't have to attach there. Their good behavior (following the rules, avoiding aggressive behavior, etc.) can be mistaken for progress and cause them to be released from the facility while their underlying attachment issues have not been resolved at all. As Caruso says, "Whether a child can navigate the mental-health system is no indicator of whether it's made a difference." At the same time, because workers at RTFs often don't understand the neurological roots of RAD, they assume that any misbehavior on the part of the children is done to annoy when really such behavior is part of their survival mechanism.

Caruso (who with her husband has adopted two children from Russia) notes that the RTFs sometimes undermine what progress has been made in the family setting because the facility's rules may differ from the family's rules. For example, one girl in an RTF was allowed to paint her fingernails as a reward for good behavior, even though the girl was not permitted to do so at home. In an ideal program, she suggests, the family and its rules and values would be incorporated as much as possible into the treatment plan, with Mom still in control. Like the funneling technique described in chapter 9, good residential programs will support the parents at every turn, rather than seeing them as part of the problem. The parents will likewise be allowed to decide on a discharge date, so that the child is released when real progress with attachment has occurred.

Insurance coverage may be a factor in the decision to send a child to an RTF and how long he or she stays there. The insurance company may hospitalize a child if it believes there is "too much liability in treating him as an outpatient," said Caruso. Insurance carriers may also limit the length of time that the child can stay in an RTF, and parents may find that this is a factor in the discharge date that the facility sets.

Respite care, either in an RTF or with therapeutic foster parents, may also be available to permit the parents and the rest of the family to "regroup" for a while when parents feel they just can't cope with the behavior anymore.

UNPROVEN "THERAPIES"

As in every field of health, some types of child "therapy" have been misapplied in untrained hands, with disastrous results. In one highly publicized case, a child died after his parents forced him to drink a vast quantity of water as a means of discipline. Another was smothered during an attempt at 'rebirthing.' One extremist school of thought urges parents to make the child so miserable physically that he or she will relinquish control.

The American Psychiatric Association (2002) states its opposition to such therapies: "While some therapists have advocated the use of so-called coercive holding therapies and/or 're-birthing techniques,' there is no scientific evidence to support the effectiveness of such interventions. In fact, there is a strong clinical consensus that coercive therapies are contraindicated in this disorder. And unfortunately, as recent events attest, such unproven and unconventional therapies can also have tragic consequences."

AN EXAMPLE OF THERAPY:
ASHLEY'S STORY

Ashley was adopted from China at age eleven months. When this little girl, not quite two years old, first took our office by storm, her two loving, intelligent, professional parents were so exhausted they could barely function. Little Ashley demanded what she wanted through grunts, pointing, or flipping regularly into "tornado" mode. Keeping up with her was exhausting and demoralizing to the parent who had been designated to stay home and frustrating beyond words to the other parent, a medical professional. Ashley's sleep "patterns" were not actually patterns in any healthy sense of the word. The entire family (both parents and an older child) was awakened regularly. No one got a good night's sleep.

Watching Ashley in the office, I wondered how this adorable but dangerously impulsive and hyperreacting (not "hyperactive" in the medical sense) whirlwind could still be alive! How was it that she hadn't darted into a busy road, fallen off a high piece of furniture, or electrocuted herself in a fit of frantic exploration by now? This is not to say that her parents weren't wonderful—quite the opposite! They were exemplary in their attempts to keep this child healthy and safe.

By the time they came to my office, they saw each of Ashley's "cute" little smiles as demonic looking, and every twist and turn of her body away from their attempts to control her felt like utter and total rejection. These loving, previously hopeful parents felt defeated and helpless, much like their child did, although she didn't have the words to describe her emotions and neurologically driven out-of-control behaviors.

Adding insult to injury for these willing-to-do-anything parents, their daughter went easily to others, not to them, for comfort, attention, and affection. This can be heartbreaking for parents. They felt (and unfortunately in many cases are right in believing) that the child had the same superficial lack of attachment to them as to anyone else who appears on the scene from whom the child felt she could get what she wanted.

My first recommendation for this family was a form of containment so that everyone knew Ashley would be safe and her mother wouldn't have to spend most of her time chasing after this child. The family started using a Mayawrap and the impact within two weeks was a powerful one. After struggling for a few days, Ashley began to realize that she couldn't get out, no matter how much she wrenched her little athletic body in every direction. Eventually she gave in and let her mother carry her everywhere. Sometimes she even stayed in the wrap at night, snuggled against Mom.

This is not a question of trying to make the child "give up." Someone once said to me, "It sounds as if you're trying to break a wild horse." Contrary to "giving up," it's a neurological "reset" button. If we are healthy at birth, we are wired to find safety and comfort in the physical presence of safe, loving parents.

Rather we are helping the child "give in." We're saying, "We know what's best for you. You must stop running around and putting yourself always in danger. Stay with me. You're okay. You're safe. Relax and let me take care of you. That's the way of nature."

So after a relatively brief struggle, born out of the realistic fear of not being well cared for, Ashley "gave in." She said, basically, "Okay, you're right, there is a place of safety in the world where I can let down my guard, where I can begin to relax, and where I can begin to retrain my overvigilant brain to slow down. Instead of always scanning for danger, I can learn how to smell the flowers. Lovely!"

Her parents described a child who, for the first time since they knew her, engaged in relaxed, sweet, gentle eye gazing and reciprocal affection.

The other major change that was happening for Ashley during this "reset" period was that she was now allowing herself to be parented. She was learning that parents, if they are strong in a positive and healthy way, do have something important to teach. Now, because she was starting to function from a physiological and psychological place of safety and a calm, alert state, she could begin to take advantage of all her parents had to offer. She was ready to catch up and move forward through normal development stages.

For Ashley, this "catch up and move forward" experience manifested itself in several dramatic ways. One was that she now showed a clear preference for her parents over others. This is critical, and not just for the issue of keeping your child safe from strangers. These little ones need to learn that their parents are the people to whom they owe their very lives. This is the critical stuff of which bonding and attachment are made—from which it evolves. Fortunately, Ashley's parents brought her in for treatment at an early age, when treatment could really make a difference.

Here is a moving account of "cuddle time" written by one of Ashley's parents:

The pressure has been building and, in a moment, the rupture happens. My daughter breaks a rule, makes a mistake, and thinks both her mother and the world are unfair. She feels the shame, she fears my reaction, and to cover the pain she screams at me in rage. And I am angry. I feel the sting.

What do I do now? Should I send her to her room, shun her briefly, make her feel the pain of isolation so she will know that this behavior is unacceptable? Will this motivate her to obedience? If I am an audience for this attack of rage, will I reinforce the behavior? I have been taught this parenting tool, this so-called "time out." Indeed, I am supposed to be an expert.

I need only look into my daughter's eyes to know that the pain she is experiencing right now is already excruciating. I can feel no desire to rub salt into her wounds with additional punishment. This seemingly small event has sent her into a downward spiral of shame. She is afraid she is unacceptable to me. She slides back to the infantile core memory of the loss of her birth mother and of her foster mother. She thought she would die then; it was a realistic fear. She carries that fear forward to this moment. She feels herself start to disintegrate, like she will cease to exist. The panic, the grieving, the rage are so powerful to her that she fears the feelings will sweep her away and tear her apart, never to return to this world.

What do I want my child to learn in this moment? If I send her to her room, she will not die. She will get over it. But at what expense? She will believe that I have sent her away because she is unacceptable to me. Or because her feelings are too big for me and I, too, am afraid of them. She will stuff all those feelings into some dark crevice of her soul. She will try to convince herself that she doesn't really need me. She will add one more concrete barrier around her heart, another lace of barbed wire. This is not what I want for my child.

I tell her that she has made a mistake, and to try not to make this mistake again. Then I sweep her up in my arms and hold her tight and close. I tell her that I love her and I need to hold her until we both feel better. She rages against my embrace. I am restraining her, holding her against her will. It takes all my strength to contain her. We are both drenched in sweat. But I am calm and my determination unwavering. The rage is eventually followed by grieving, and then finally by calm. We snuggle and whisper and giggle, and all is well in the world again. We are connected, our souls touching. And this is what my daughter learns: "I will hold you for as long as it takes. Though you would cut me with the razor shards of your shattered soul, I will sweep up the pieces and be the glue that holds you together. I will be your lifeboat and we will ride the waves of your rage and panic and pain together. Your feelings do not scare me. I will help you with them. I will not abandon you. I am your mother. I am powerful, unwavering, permanent and safe. My love is unconditional."

Afterwards, my daughter is calm, centered and obedient. She follows the rules because she wants to. She knows she is safe and loved. We Quakers have an expression about holding. When someone is hurting or in need, we "hold them in the Light." This is how I hold my daughter in the Light. This is my direct experience of God.

11

CONCLUSION

Adoption is the forming of a lasting relationship, claiming as your own a child who is not genetically connected to you. Adoptions are much like marriages: some thrive, some fail, and some are mediocre. It can be said that the attachment process in adoption simulates what happens when infants and parents attach to each other, and what happens when adults fall in love and make a lifelong commitment to marriage. Both involve a courtship, a time of getting to know each other.

—NORMA FINNELL

In the preceding chapters I hope that I have given you a picture of how to promote healthy attachments, what attachment problems look like, and how problems of attaching can be prevented (as best as we can) and treated. I have seen some wonderful successes as parents and children attach and become healthy families. It is personally and professionally gratifying to see my clients' hard work in therapy as it brings fulfillment to them and their families. What a thrill it is for me when these children make breakthroughs!

In this book you've read harrowing stories about some children with serious problems. You've also read some heartwarming accounts of how wonderful successful attachment can be. My goal in writing this book has not been to discourage parents from adopting, but rather to show you what can sometimes happen and to share information and suggestions so that you can take every possible step to enhance attachment with your child. I want parents to be well prepared for what may happen and aware that you may need to practice a different kind of parenting to be successful.

What does the future hold for children who come into adoptive families with attachment issues? Problems of attachment and their behavioral manifestations can rear their ugly heads at stressful times throughout a person's life. Anniversaries and milestones can be a particularly risky time (for example, birthdays and anniversaries of separation from birth parents). So can developmental stages, such as puberty or leaving home. On going to college, for example, an adolescent may be troubled by the same old questions that plagued him in his earlier days: "What if nobody likes me? What if I'm lonely?" Almost all of us have had those feelings and thoughts before. But for the child with attachment problems in his or her history, this may be a highly exaggerated, even dangerous experience.

When a woman who had attachment problems as a child gives birth, for instance, all her old insecurities can come back to haunt her. She needs more reassurance than the average mother that all new mothers and fathers have a lot of questions and doubts about themselves at this point. But she may also need the extra reassurance that even though her own attachment process was not ideal, her attachment with her baby can be strong and healthy, with patience, guidance, and support.

Adoption has been around since the beginning of time. However, the treatment of attachment problems is still in its infancy. Therapists for attachment problems are doing cutting-edge work, using information from current medical and psychological research, traditional and new treatment methods, and safe clinical judgment and putting them together in exciting, meaningful ways. Interweaving many therapy approaches, such as those described in the previous chapter, and collaborating with mental health professionals, occupational and physical therapists, physicians, massage therapists, school professionals, and child welfare workers, as well as juvenile justice professionals and others, can provide for the maximum therapeutic benefit to children and adolescents (and their families) who have been suffering needlessly for lack of appropriate care.

When searching for help, be sure to find someone who can apply all the available techniques to help you and your child successfully identify and treat attachment issues. Many practitioners learn and employ only one or perhaps two types of therapies, hoping either or both will cure the problem. But a good attachment and trauma therapist will carefully combine numbers of appropriate therapies into a network of interventions. He or she will always work with the family and continuously evaluate progress and needs for adjustments in interventions. Such therapists will stay on top of the latest research about the children and adolescents they treat and why their rehabilitation and healing can be so resistant. We are learning why we often cannot rely on one or two methods of intervention: these children's brains are complicated! Many have developed in ways that render them highly resistant to healing. The good news is that by combining sound psychological theory and practice with new brain research we are helping children heal from their traumatic pasts. The alternative is to continue to see these children show up in disproportionate numbers in mental hospitals, the criminal justice system, special education classes, and detention centers. Our infrastructure—insurance companies, school districts, health and mental health professionals, and the legal system—needs to be open and responsive to new information about the ways our minds and bodies and behaviors work together and influence each other. Bureaucratic roadblocks and disagreements among academic professionals mean that treatment for some children may actually be going backwards.

I hope the field will open its heart, mind, and eyes to the needs of these children. More and more research (e.g., Anda et al. 2002; Van der Kolk et al. 1996) supports the finding that if we do not intervene early to treat and heal emotional trauma, the results in human misery and monetary costs are tremendous. It is my hope and dream that through works such as this book and groups such as ATTACh, new understanding on the part of adoption agencies, orphanages, and similar institutions, and through general education that enlightens and supports us all, we will prevent many of the problems we are now trying to treat. I invite you to please share with us your experiences, what you have learned, and how we can help to share your loving attachment with your little one. Please visit our website at www.instituteforchildren.com, and know that my best wishes for a happy, healthy life are with you all!

PARENTING PROFILE FOR DEVELOPING ATTACHMENT

Respond from 1 (very little) to 5 (very much) Focus on the adult's abilities, not whether or not the child is receptive to the interaction.

	My Perception of Self	My Perception of Spouse/ Friend
1. Able to maintain a sense of humor		
2. Comfortable with giving physical affection		
3. Comfortable receiving physical affection		
4. Ready to comfort child in distress		

	My Perception of Self	My Perception of Spouse/ Friend
5. Able to be playful with child	_____	_____
6. Ready to listen to child's thoughts and feelings	_____	_____
7. Able to be calm and relaxed much of the time	_____	_____
8. Patient with child's mistakes	_____	_____
9. Patient with child's misbehaviors	_____	_____
10. Patient with child's anger and defiance	_____	_____
11. Patient with child's primary two symptoms	_____	_____
12. Comfortable expressing love for child	_____	_____
13. Able to show empathy for child's distress	_____	_____
14. Able to show empathy for child's anger	_____	_____
15. Able to set limits, with empathy, not anger	_____	_____
16. Able to give consequences, regardless of his response	_____	_____

	My Perception of Self	My Perception of Spouse/ Friend
17. Able and willing to give child much supervision	_____	_____
18. Able and willing to give child much "mom time"	_____	_____
19. Able to express anger in a quick, to-the-point manner	_____	_____
20. Able to "get over it" quickly after conflict with child	_____	_____
21. Able to allow child to accept consequence of choice	_____	_____
22. Able to accept, though not necessarily agree with, the thoughts and feelings of your child	_____	_____
23. Able to accept, though you may still discipline, the behavior of your child	_____	_____
24. Able to receive support from other adults in raising this difficult child	_____	_____
25. Able to acknowledge failings and mistakes in raising this difficult child	_____	_____

	My Perception of Self	My Perception of Spouse/ Friend
26. Able to ask for help from people you trust	_____	_____
27. Able to refrain from allowing your child's problems from becoming your problems	_____	_____
28. Able to cope with criticism from other adults about how you raise your child	_____	_____
29. Able to avoid experiencing shame and rage over your failures to help your child	_____	_____
30. Able to remain focused on the long-term goals	_____	_____

From http://danielhughes.homestead.com (used by permission).

APPENDIX B

RESOURCES

ORGANIZATIONS/HELPFUL WEBSITES

Association for Treatment and Training in the Attachment of
    Children (ATTACh)
www.ATTACh.org

Autism Network International
(ANI)
www.students.uiuc.edu/~bordner/nai.html

Behavenet
www.behavenet.com

BrainPlace.com
www.brainplace.com

ChildTrauma.org
www.childtrauma.org

Child Welfare League of America
www.cwla.org

EEG Spectrum
www.eegspectrum.com

Homes for Kids
www.homes4kids.org

Home School Legal Defense Association
www.hslda.org

Daniel Hughes
dhughes@pivot.net

National Center for Home Education
www.nche@nslda.org

The International Society for Neuronal Regulation
www.isnr.org

The Brian Othmer Foundation
www.brianothmer.org

Nancy Spoolstra
www.radzebra.org

Theraplay®
www.theraplay.org

Voice for Adoption
(202) 543-7372

Mayawrap©
www.mayawrap.com

BOOKS/VIDEOS/OTHER PUBLICATIONS

I Love You Rituals
By Becky A. Baily, Ph.D.

OTHER WORKS BY BECKY BAILY:

CD/Cassette:
Songs for I Love You Rituals
10 Principles of Positive Discipline
Preventing Power Struggles
Transforming Aggression into Healthy Self-Esteem
Brain Smart
Conflict Resolution

Video:
Touch a Heart, Teach a Mind: The Brain-Smart Way to Build Bonds

Books:
Easy to Love, Difficult to Discipline
Conscious Discipline: Brain Smart Classroom Management for Elementary Schools
Shubert's BIG Voice

www.beckybaily.com

Every Child Needs (video)
Production of WTTW Chicago
Robert R. McCormick Tribune Foundation, 1997

What You Should Know Before You Adopt a Child
By The Attachment Center at Evergreen, Inc.
P.O. Box 2764
Evergreen, Colorado 80437-2764
(303) 674-1910

GLOSSARY

504 accommodations: 504 plans, based on civil rights legislation as contained in the Vocational Rehabilitation Act of 1973, are intended to ensure that disabilities do not interfere with access to education. 504 accommodations typically require modifications to the learning environment and modifications to adult responses to behavior.

Apgar scale (Apgar score): A practical method to assess a newborn infant's health, the Apgar score is a number arrived at by scoring the heart rate, respiratory effort, muscle tone, skin color, and response to a catheter in the nostril. Each of these objective signs can receive 0, 1, or 2 points. An Apgar score of 10 means an infant is in the best possible condition. The Apgar score is done routinely sixty seconds after the complete birth of the infant. An infant with a score of 0-3 needs immediate resuscitation. The Apgar score is commonly repeated five minutes after birth and, in the event of a difficult resuscitation, may be done again at ten, fifteen, and twenty minutes.

Attachment: Attachment is a reciprocal process by which an emotional connection develops between an infant and his or her primary caregiver. It influences the child's physical, neurological, cognitive, and psychological development. It becomes the basis for development of basic trust and shapes how the child will relate to the world, learn, and form relationships throughout life.

Attachment disorder: Attachment disorder is a significant dysfunction in an individual's ability to trust or engage in reciprocal loving, lasting relationships. An attachment disorder may occur after a traumatic disruption in the caregiver-child bond during the first years of life. It can distort future stages of development and increase the risk of other serious emotional and behavioral problems, but is also treatable. For a medical definition of *Reactive Attachment Disorder* of Infancy or Early Childhood 313.89, see the *Diagnostic and Statistical Manual IV-TR.*

Attachment therapist: The attachment therapist is a professional who will work with children and primary caregivers to promote healthy attachment. The therapist should be trained in attachment theory and child development, be able to practice interventions that meet ATTACh's safety standards, teach parents good attachment skills, and work with extended family and schools as needed. Therapy should focus on the attachment relationship, not on the child's symptoms, and the therapist should support the authority and values of the parents.

Attunement: Attunement is a powerful emotional connection in which the caregiver recognizes, connects with, and shares the child's inner states (Stern, 1985). The caregiver's attuned response then matches the child's expression in a complementary form of intensity and expression. It is the experience of "feeling *with* rather than feeling for" (McWilliams, 1994).

Autonomous/secure attachment style (or state of mind with regard to attachment): An adult attachment style wherein the person feels both self-confident and firmly connected to significant others in his life, usually owing to secure early childhood attachments.

Cognitive dissonance: A psychological conflict resulting from incongruous beliefs and attitudes held simultaneously.

Disorganized/disoriented attachment style (or state of mind with regard to attachment): In early childhood, an insecure attachment style characterized by aimless, chaotic behavior by the child in the presence of primary caregivers.

Dysregulation: A lack of proper regulation; an inability of the brain to maintain appropriate flexibility or stability.

"Fight, flight, or freeze": A response of the brain to danger that motivates someone to attack, escape from, or try to make themselves "invisible" to the source of danger. Children with attachment disorder may have the "fight, flight, or freeze" response to normal stimuli, leading to behavior problems and impaired development.

Holding: A therapeutic technique that includes eye contact, appropriate touch, empathy, genuine expression of emotion, nurturance, and reciprocity to create a feeling of safety, trust, and acceptance. While a variety of holding positions can be used, the physical safety of the client is the primary consideration.

Hyperarousal: A state of elevated or increased alertness, awareness, or wakefulness (for more on hyperarousal and other behavior states, see www.behavenet.com).

Hypervigilance: An enhanced state of sensory sensitivity accompanied by an exaggerated intensity of behaviors whose purpose it is to detect threats.

Impaired attachment style: The characteristic way in which a child or adult with a history of insecure attachments approaches new relationships, such that the new attachments are also likely to be insecure.

Insecure/avoidant attachment style (or state of mind with regard to attachment): An adult attachment style wherein the person experiences unfulfilling close relationships due to her tendency to remain physically or emotionally distant, often preceded by avoidant attachments in early childhood.

Mayawrap: A baby sling and pouch carrier that keeps you in direct contact with your baby for constant bonding.

Plasticity in the brain: The remarkable capacity of the brain to change its molecular, microarchitectural, and functional organization in response to injury or experience.

Preoccupied attachment style (or state of mind with regard to attachment): An adult attachment style wherein the person frequently experiences anxiety in close relationships, vacillating between feeling uncomfortably close or uncomfortably distant, often preceded by resistant attachments during childhood.

Self-soothing: Behaviors such as thumb-sucking and rocking that help the child to transition from feelings of anxiety or nervousness to a more calm, relaxed state.

Sensory bath: The sensory input (of touch, movement, smell, etc.) that in early childhood releases a pattern of neuronal activity that is crucial to development.

Traumatic event: An event in which a person experiences or witnesses actual or threatened death or physical harm (to himself or others), leading to feelings of intense fear, helplessness, or horror. In children, this may be expressed instead by disorganized or agitated behavior.

Unresolved-with-regard-to-attachment style (or state of mind with regard to attachment): An adult attachment style wherein the person tends to experience chaotic, insecure relationships, often preceded by disorganized/disoriented attachments during childhood.

Weighted vest: A vest similar to that used in the dentist's office when X-rays are taken. The weight of the vest is often helpful and comforting to the child when he is trying to relax.

BIBLIOGRAPHY

Ainsworth, Mary (1978). *Patterns of Attachment: A Psychological Study of the Strange Situation*. New York: Random House.

Amen, Daniel (1998). *Change Your Brain, Change Your Life*. New York: Times Books.

Amen, Daniel (2002). *Healing the Hardware of the Soul*. New York: Free Press.

Amen, Daniel (2003). Amen Brain System Check List. www.brainplace.com.

American Psychiatric Association (2000). *Diagnostic and Statistical Manual IV-TR*. Washington, D.C.: American Psychiatric Association.

American Psychiatric Association (2002). Reactive Attachment Disorder Position Statement. APA Document #200205. www.apa.org. Accessed October 2002.

Anda, Robert, S. Dube, V. Felitti, V. Edwards, and D. Williamson (2002). Exposure to Abuse, Neglect, and Household Dysfunction among Adults Who Witnessed Intimate Partner Violence as Children: Implications of Health and Social Services. *Violence and Victims* 17 (1): 3–17.

Anda, Robert, V. J. Felliti, D. P. Chapman, et al. (2001). Abused boys, battered mothers, and male involvement in teen pregnancy. *Pediatrics* 107 (2): E19.

ATTACh (Association for Treatment and Training in the Attachment of Children) (2003). www.attach.org.

Bailey, Becky A. (2000). *I Love You Rituals*. Harper Collins: New York.

Bascom, Barbara, and Carole McKelvery (1997). *The Complete Guide to Foreign Adoption: What to Expect and How to Prepare for Your New Child*. New York: Pocket Books.

Beauvais-Godwin, L., and R. Godwin (1997). *The Complete Adoption Book*. Holbrook, Mass.: Adams Media.

BehaveNet. www.behave.com. Accessed July 31, 2003.

Bettelheim, Bruno (1989). *The Uses of Enchantment: The Meaning and Importance of Fairy Tales*. New York: Random House.

Blair, Clancey (2002). School Readiness: Integrating Cognition and Emotion in a Neurobiological Conceptualization of Children's Functioning at School Entry. *American Psychologist* 57 (2): 111–127.

Bloom, Sandra (2002). *The PVS Disaster: Poverty, Violence and Substance Abuse in the Lives of Women and Children*. Philadelphia: Women's Law Project.

Blum, Deborah (2002). *Love at Goon Park*. Cambridge, Mass.: Perseus.

Booth, Phyllis (2002). Theraplay Principles Help Attachment Parenting. *Connections ATTACh*, August: 2-3.

Bowlby, John (1988). *A Secure Base: Parent-Child Attachment and Healthy Human Development*. New York: Basic Books.

Brazelton, T. Berry (1992). *Touch Points: Your Child's Emotional and Behavioral Development*. New York: Merloyd Lawrence.

Briere, John (1996). *Trauma Symptom Checklist for Children*. Odessa, Fla.: Psychological Assessment Resources.

Brodzinsky, David M., Marshall D. Schechter, and Robin Marantz Henig (1993). *Being Adopted: The Lifelong Search for Self*. New York: Anchor.

Brodzinsky, David M., Daniel Smith, and Anne Brodzinsky (1998). *Children's Adjustment to Adoption: Developmental and Clinical Issues*. Thousand Oaks, Calif.: Sage.

Calhoun, C., and P. Resnick (1993). Chapter 2. In D. H. Barlow, ed., *Clinical Handbook of Psychological Disorders: A Step-by-Step Treatment Manual*, 2d ed. Albany: State University of New York.

Canfield, Ken (1996). *The Heart of a Father: How Dads Can Shape The Destiny of America*. Chicago: Northfield Publishing.

Carter, Mildred, and Tammy Weber (1994). *Body Reflexology: Healing at Your Fingertips*, rev. and updated ed. West Nyack, N.Y.: Parker.

Caruso, Kathy (2002). Personal communication.

Child Trauma Academy. www.childtrauma.org. Accessed August 7, 2003.

Cline, Foster, and Jin Fay (1992). *Parenting with Love and Logic*. Colorado Springs, Colo.: Pinon.

Cognitive Behavioral Therapy. www.cognitive-behavior-therapy.org. Accessed August 3, 2003.

Eshleman, Christopher Ross (2002, 2003). Personal communication.

Eshleman, John D. (2002). Personal communication.

Eshleman, Lark (2000). *Healing Emotional Trauma: Treating the Wounded Child*. Lancaster, Pa.: Acorn Press.

Eshleman, Lark (2001). *Attachment Disorder: Solving the Puzzle*. West Chester, Pa.: CVP Communications.

Eshleman, Lark (2003). Behaviors of Children and Adolescents Affected by Reactive Attachment Disorder of Infancy or Early Childhood. Monograph Checklist.

Fahlberg, Vera (1991). *A Child's Journey through Placement*. Indianapolis: Perspectives.

Finnell, Norma (1996). Adoption and Attachment. *Theraplay Institute Newsletter* (Fall).

Flanders, Gary (2002). Personal communication.

Gannon, M.J., and associates (1994). *Understanding Global Cultures: Metaphorical Journeys through 17 countries*. Thousand Oaks, Calif.: Sage.

Garbarino, J. (1999). *Lost Boys: Why Our Sons Turn Violent and How We Can Save Them*. New York: Anchor Books.

Garbarino, J., Kathleen Kastelny, and Nancy Dubrow (1991). *No Place To Be A Child: Growing Up in a War Zone*. San Francisco: Jossey-Bass.

Garbarino, J., and Frances Stott (1992). *What Children Can Tell Us: Eliciting, Interpreting and Evaluating Critical Information from Children*. San Francisco: Jossey-Bass.

BIBLIOGRAPHY

Gardner, Richard (1988). *Psychotherapy with Adolescents*. New Jersey: Creative Therapeutics.

Goff, Elizabeth (2002, 2003). Personal communication.

Gray, Lauren (2002, 2003). Personal communication.

Guterl, F. (2002). What Freud Got Right. *Newsweek*, November 11, pp. 50–51.

Hagen, Matthew C., Jose V. Pardo, David H. Zald, and Tricia A. Thorton (2002). Somatosensory Processing in the Human Inferior Prefrontal Cortex. *Journal of Neurophysiology* 88 (November): 1400–1406.

Hallowell, E. (2002). *The Childhood Roots of Adult Happiness: Five Steps to Help Kids Create and Sustain Lifelong Joy*. New York: Ballantine.

Harris, Judith (1998). *The Nurture Assumption: Why Children Turn Out The Way They Do*. New York: Simon & Schuster.

Hill, Robert, and Eduardo Castro (2002). *Getting Rid of Ritalin: How Neurofeedback Can Successfully Treat Attention Deficit Disorder without Drugs*. Charlottesville, Va.: Hampton Roads.

Hindman, Molly (2003). Personal communication.

Hochman, Gloria (2003). All That's Clear Is Pain, *Philadelphia Inquirer*, March 15, 2003.

Hughes, Daniel (1997). *Facilitating Developmental Attachment*. Northvale, N.J.: Jason Aronson.

Hughes, Daniel (1998). *Building the Bonds of Attachment: Awakening Love in Deeply Troubled Children*. Northvale, N.J.: Jason Aronson.

"Jade" (2002). Personal communication.

Jaffe, P., D. Wolfe, S. K. Wilson, and L. Zak (1986). Family Violence and Child Adjustment: A Comparative Analysis of Girls' and Boys' Behavioral Symptoms. *American Journal of Psychiatry* 143 (1): 74-76.

Jernberg, A., A. Allert, T. Koller, and P. Booth (1983). *Reciprocity in Parent-Infant Relationships*. Chicago: Theraplay Institute.

Karr-Morse, Robin, and Meredith Wiley (1997). *Ghosts from the Nursery: Tracing the Roots of Violence*. New York: Atlantic Monthly Press.

Keck, G., and Regina Kupecky (2002). *Parenting the Hurt Child: Helping Adoptive Families Heal and Grow*. Colorado Springs, Colo.: Pinon.

Kelly, Joe (2002). Excerpted from Families with Children from China website (www.fccny.org).

Kelly, V. J. (2003). *Theoretical Rationale for Attachment Therapy*. Columbia, S.C.: Association for Treatment and Training in the Attachment of Children.

Kroll, J. (1993). *PTSD/Borderlines in Therapy: Finding the Balance*. New York: Norton.

Levine, Peter (1999). *How to Heal Trauma through Your Body*. Audiotape Series. Boulder, Colo.: Sounds True.

Lindaman, Sandra (1996). Theraplay for Adopted Children. *Adoption Therapist* 7 (1).

Main, M., and Solomon, J. (1986). Discovery of an Insecure Disorganized/Disoriented Attachment Pattern: Procedures, Findings and Implications for Classification of Behaviour. In M. Yogman and T. B. Brazelton, *Affective Development in Infancy*. Norwood, N.J.: Ablex, pp. 95-124.

McKelvey, Carole A., ed. (1995) *Give Them Roots, Then Let Them Fly: Understanding Attachment Therapy*. Evergreen, Colo.: Attachment Center Press.

McMullin, Rian (1986). *Handbook of Cognitive Therapy Techniques*. New York: Norton.

McWilliams, N. (1994). *Psychoanalytic Diagnosis: Understanding Personality Structure in the Clinical Process*. New York: Guilford.

Minuchin, S. (1974). *Families and Family Therapy*. Cambridge, Mass.: Harvard University Press.

Moyer, A. (2002). Personal communication.

Moyer, B. (2002, 2003). Personal communication.

Nature's Babies: Animal Families. Videotape. Cerritos, Calif.: Diamond Entertainment.

Osofsky, J. D. (1999). The impact of violence on children. *Future Child* 9(3): 33-49.

Ozalas, Joelle (2002). Personal communication.

Perry, Bruce (2001, 2002). http://www.childtrauma.org. Accessed November 20, 2002.

Perry, Bruce (1997). In *Ten Things Every Child Needs* (videotape). Chicago: WTTW Chicago and The Chicago Production Center.

Randolph, Elizabeth (1999). *Children Who Shock and Surprise: A Guide to Attachment Disorder*, 3rd ed.

Randolph, Elizabeth (1999). *Children Who Shock and Surprise: A Guide to Attachment Disorder*, 3rd ed. Hillsborough, N.J.: Tapestry Books.

Rhodes, R. (1999). *Why They Kill*. New York: Knopf.

Robbins, Jim (1996). Wired for Miracles. *Psychology Today*, March/April.

Robbins, Jim (2000). *A Symphony in the Brain: The Evolution of the New Brain Wave Biofeedback*. Boston: Atlantic Monthly Press.

Robert R. McCormick Tribune Foundation (1997). *Ten Things Every Child Needs*. Videotape. Chicago: WTTW Chicago and the Chicago Production Center.

Rothschild, B. (2000). *The Body Remembers Casebook: Unifying Methods and Models in the Treatment of Trauma and PTSD*. New York: Norton.

Satir, Virginia (1988). *The New Peoplemaking*. Mountain View, Calif.: Science and Behavior Books.

Schore, A. N. (2002). Dysregulation of the Right Brain: A Fundamental Mechanism of Traumatic Attachment and the Psychopathogenesis of Stress Disorder. *Australia and New Zealand Journal of Psychiatry*, February: 9–30.

Shapiro, Francine (1998). *EMDR: The Breakthrough Therapy for Overcoming Anxiety, Stress, and Trauma*. New York: Basic Books.

Sherman, R., and N. Friedman (1986). *Handbook of Structured Techniques in Marriage and Family Therapy*. New York: Brunner/Mazel.

Siegel, Daniel (1999). *The Developing Mind: Toward a Neurobiology of Interpersonal Experience*. New York: Guilford.

Stern, D. N. (1985). *The Interpersonal World of the Infant*. New York: Basic Books.

Tardibuono, John (2002, 2003). Personal communication.

Thomas, Nancy (1997). *When Love Is Not Enough: A Guide to Parenting Children with Reactive Attachment Disorder*. Glenwood Springs, Colo.: Nancy L. Thomas.

Van der Kolk, B., A. McFarlane, and L. Weisaeth, eds. (1996). *Traumatic Stress: The Effects of Overwhelming Experience on Mind, Body and Society*. New York: Guilford.

Welch, Martha (1988). *Holding Time*. New York: Simon & Schuster.

INDEX

abuses, physical and emotional, 18

"acting out" daily situations, 152

adoption: reasons for, xii–xiii; concern about, 5; starting attachment process before, 55–56

adverse childhood experiences (ACE), 48

advice from parents without adopted children, 80, 86

affection, 94, 152

age, 19, 37, 97, 110, 121, 149; emotional vs. chronological, 37, 110, 150

Ainsworth, Mary, 13–14, 30–31

allergic reactions, 57, 58, 110

American Psychiatric Association, 135, 156, 157. *See also Diagnostic and Statistical Manual IV-R*

animal kingdom, 23–24

Apgar Scale, 6

assessment. *See* diagnosis of attachment disorders

ATTACh (Association for Treatment and Training in the Attachment of Children), xv, 26–27, 42, 43, 136

attachment: activities to enhance, 94–99; in animal kingdom, 23–24; ATTACh's definition of, 43; basics of fostering, 81–82; bonding as, 6–7; common behaviors of, 30–31; definition of, 26–27; first-year cycle, 7; and medical care, 110; in newborns, 24–26; progress in, 67, 102–3; promotion at home, 70–73; and Rs, Ps, and Cs, 151; through teaching of social cues, 93–94; timetable for, 69, 71–72

attachment disorder, 4–6, 8, 9, 39, 42, 65, 121–23. *See also* reactive attachment disorder (RAD)

Attachment Disorder: Solving the Puzzle, xv

attachment issues, 9, 47–48, 163

attachment styles, 13–18

attachment theory, 11–16, 18–21

attachment therapy, 49–52, 61–62, 103–5, 133, 138–40, 157–61, 163–64

attention, measure of, 144–45

attention deficit hyperactivity disorder (ADHD), 137

attunement, 25–26, 67, 74

audiotapes, from country of origin, 59

Australia and New Zealand Journal of Psychiatry, 48

autism, 137

autonomous/secure style, 19–20

babies, responses of, 73–74
baby products, 57–58
Balkans, xiv
basically dysregulated, 74
Bettelheim, Bruno, 27
Biever, John, xvi
biofeedback, 143–46
Blair, Clancey, 116
body parts, naming, 99
bonding, 6–7, 25–26, 55–56, 65, 68–69, 87–88
Booth, Phyllis, 26, 149, 150
Bowlby, John, 13, 29, 30, 36
brain, 39, 83, 144–48, 152. *See also* neurology
Brain Gym, 154
brain plasticity, 15–16
brainwave biofeedback, 143–46

Calhoun, C., 139–40
calm alert, 40, 117, 145
Cambodia, 111
Camp Celebration, 151–53
caregiver, primary, 6–7, 16–17, 26
caregivers, 17, 19–20, 73
Caruso, Julie, 156
Cassatt, Mary, 23
cheating in school, 123
child development, 12, 16–18
child proofing, 57
children, thought processes of, 82–85
Child Study Center, Fort Worth, 152
China, 111
choices, limited, 90
clothing, 58–59
coercive therapies, 157
cognitive behavioral therapy (CBT), 153
cognitive dissonance, 99, 141
cognitive function, 153
consequences for poor behavior, 129
containment, structure and, 90

control issues, 116, 139
cortisol, elevated levels of, 29
Cross, David, 153
cruelty, 152
crying, 73–74, 86–87

dental care, 61
desensitization, systematic, 100, 142–43
"Desert Storm," 83–85
despair, 13, 36
detachment, 13
The Developing Mind (Siegel), 39, 83
developmental level, awareness of, 19
developmental skills, 61
Diagnostic and Statistical Manual IV-R, 9
diagnosis of attachment disorder, 136–138
discipline, in school, 129
disorganized/disoriented style, 14–15
dysregulated, 74
doctors, 110–12, 155
dreams, bad, 83

education, 115–133
EEG biofeedback, 143–46
EMDR (eye movement desensitization and reprocessing), 146–49
emotional age. *See* age
emotional dysfunction, 153
engagement, in Theraplay, 149
eye contact, 143

father, 6
fears, 67, 83–85, 97, 101–2, 142–43. *See also* fight, flight, or freeze mode
Feldenkrais, 154
fight, flight, or freeze mode, 36–39, 116, 122, 142
"first attacher," 71–72
first-year attachment cycle, 7, 25–26

504 accommodations, 128–30
Flanders, Gary, 111, 120–21, 130–33
food, 60–61, 152
food hoarding, 152
Freud, Sigmund, 12, 13
frustration tolerance, 17
fun and love, 90, 150
funneling technique, 118–19, 129, 156

games, baby, 96–97, 151
Goff, Elizabeth, 67, 68–69, 71, 73–74,
    86–87, 102–3, 111
Guatemala, 111

Harlow, Harry, 24
Harmann, Mark, 58
*Healing from Emotional Trauma:
    Treating the Wounded Child*
    (Eshleman), xiv
health care. *See* medical care
help from others, 69
heritage, preservation of, 75–79
hide-and-seek, 97
homecoming, 65–73. *See also* transition
home schooling, 120
"honeymoon period," 69–70
hospitalization, 155–57
house, preparation of, 56–57
Hughes, Daniel, 87, 89–90, 151
Hutchinson, Bill, 93
hygiene, poor, 123
hyperarousal, 29
hyperreactive behavior, 36, 142–43
hypervigilant mode, 8–9, 36–39, 100,
    116

I Love You Rituals, 95
impulsivity, measure of, 144–45
independence, 16
individualized education programs
    (IEPs), 123–28
inpatient treatment, 155–57

insecure/avoidant style, 14–15
insecure/resistant style, 14–15
instincts, 23–26
Institute for Children and Families
    (ICF), xiv
insurance, 112–14, 141, 155–57
integrated awareness, 154
interdependencies, 16–18
international adoption, 20–21, 56,
    65–73, 109–14

Keck, Greg, 100
Kelly, Joe, 28
Kupecky, Regina, 100

least restrictive environment, 126–27
love, 90, 150
lying, 152

Main, Mary, 13–14
manners, poor, 123
Mayawrap, 58
medical care, 72–73, 109–14
medications, 111, 154–55
mental health professionals, 135–38,
    143, 164
mental illness, 14, 15, 18, 34
misbehavior, 91–93, 98, 121–23, 156
Mom, 6–7, 16–17, 26
music, 58
music therapy, 154

natural order, 31
Nature's Babies: Animal Families, 24
nature vs. nurture, 23–24
neglect, 35–37, 39–42
neurofeedback, 143–46
neurology, 28–29, 36, 83. *See also* brain
newborns, 24–26
nicknames, 95
normal behavior, 29–32
nurturing, 23–24, 149–50

occupational therapy, 154
oppositional defiant disorder, 137

parenting, 86–89, 110. *See also* reparenting; testimonies, by parents
Parenting the Hurt Child (Keck and Kupecky), 100
parents, 5, 19, 81–82, 120
Parents' Network for Post-Institutionalized Children, 152
"pass the baby," 66, 67–68
Patterson, Bob, 145–46
pediatrician appointments, 72–73, 110
peekaboo, 97, 143
Perry, Bruce, 27
photographs, from country of origin, 59
physical closeness, 68, 74, 89, 90, 110
physical therapy, 154
planned regression, 87, 90
plasticity of the brain, 15
positive talk, 98, 141. *See also* funneling technique
posttraumatic stress disorder, 4, 39
praise. *See* positive talk
products, to enhance attachment, 57–58
protest, 13
psychiatric treatment, 112–14
psychotherapy, 15–16, 112–14
Purvis, Karyn, 152, 153

reactive attachment disorder (RAD), 3, 9, 35–39, 42–48, 135–38. *See also* attachment disorder
"reading" your child, 91–93, 110
rebirthing, 157
regression, 87, 88, 153
rejection, 87–88
reparenting, 151. *See also* parenting
Resnick, P., 139–40

residential treatment facilities (RTFs), 155–57
restoration and repair, 17
Romania, 111
routine, 90, 96, 118
Russia, 111

safety: children's perception of, 41–42; and EMDR, 148–49; and environment for asking questions, 85; lack of, 36–37; need for, 26–28; and neurology, 28–29; and parenting, 88–89; and physical closeness, 74, 90; and reparenting, 151; and systematic desensitization, 142
school, 119–23. *See also* individualized education programs (IEPs); school districts; teachable moments; teachers; teaching
school districts, 115–16, 127–30
school nurses, 122
school staff, 120–23, 126–27
Schore, A. N., 48
secure attachment style, 14
Seidel, Kathie, 153
self-concept, 87, 99–100, 141
self-injury, 122
self-regulation, 28, 92, 116–17, 122, 145
self-soothing, 17, 122
sensory bath, 68
sensory stimulation, 151
separations, temporary, 100–102
Shapiro, Francine, 146
siblings, 70
Siegel, Daniel, 39, 83
similarity finding, 95–96
sleeping, 73, 86
smells, 72
social contracts, 152
social cues, 93–94, 97
Songs for I Love You Rituals, 58

sounds, 58–60. *See also* speaking
sound therapies, 154
speaking, 94–95. *See also* positive talk
states of mind with regard to attach-
    ment, 14–15
stealing, 123, 152
"stranger practice," 152
stress, chronic, 110
structure, 90, 149
supervision, 90, 122–23
symptoms of attachment disorders. *See*
    diagnosis of attachment disorders
synergistic trauma and attachment
    therapy, 140–41

tabula rasa, 12
Tardibuono, John, 82–83
Texas Christian University, 152
teachable moments, 117
teachers, 120–23, 130–33
teaching, 117–19
team building, 97–98
tease-free zone, 99
terminology, 9
testimonies, by parents, 10, 49–52,
    61–62, 75–79, 103–105, 112–114,
    133, 157–161
therapists. *See* mental health
    professionals

therapy, 134–161
Theraplay, 95, 149–51
Theraplay Institute, 149
Tocqueville, Alexis de, xii–xiii
toilet-training, 88
touch, 143
TOVA (test of variables of attention),
    144–45
toys, 58
transition, 58–61, 64–65, 71–73.
    See also homecoming
trauma, 37–42, 148. *See also* synergistic
    trauma and attachment therapy
trauma-reduction therapy, 51
Trauma Symptom Checklist for
    Children, 137–38
traumatic events, 37–38
trust, 35–37, 40–41, 66, 82, 92,
    99–100, 140, 153

"unconditional being with," 68
United States Surgeon General, 34

videotapes, from country of origin, 59
Vietnam, 111
volatile organic chemicals (VOCs),
    57

Welch, Martha, 40

ABOUT THE AUTHOR

Lark Eshleman, Ph.D., and is the founder and director of the Institute for Children and Families. A psychotherapist, Dr. Eshleman has trained orphanage workers in Croatia to work with children before they are adopted. A frequent speaker and writer on emotional trauma and attachment issues, she lives in West Chester, Pennsylvania.